A
New
England
Love
Story

A NEW ENGLAND LOVE STORY

Nathaniel Hawthorne and Sophia Peabody

by LouAnn Gaeddert

THE DIAL PRESS · NEW YORK

920
G

Published by
The Dial Press
1 Dag Hammarskjold Plaza
New York, New York 10017

Copyright © 1980 by LouAnn Gaeddert
Design by Holly McNeely
First printing

Library of Congress Cataloging in Publication Data

Gaeddert, LouAnn Bigge.
A New England love story.

Bibliography: p.
Summary: Relates the love story of
Nathaniel Hawthorne and Sophia Peabody
based on their letters and journals.
1. Hawthorne, Nathaniel, 1804–1864—
Biography—Marriage. 2. Hawthorne,
Sophia Amelia Peabody, 1811–1871.
3. Novelists, American—19th century—
Biography. 4. Wives—United States—
Biography. [1. Hawthorne, Nathaniel,
1804–1864. 2. Hawthorne, Sophia Amelia
Peabody, 1811–1871. 3. Authors, American.
4. Artists] I. Title.
PS1882.G3   813'.3   [B]   [920]   80–16329
ISBN 0-8037-6153-8

FOR ORLAN

Contents

A
New
England
Love
Story

Prologue

Some say that as late as 1837 ghosts hovered over the seaport of Salem, Massachusetts. They were the spirits of women who, more than a century earlier, had been convicted of witchcraft and hanged on Gallows Hill just outside of the city.

The ghosts must have gloated over a grim old house on Herbert Street, for in it lived three eccentric descendants of one of the judges responsible for the hangings. The house was turned sideways on its narrow lot and the pathway to the door was almost overgrown with straggly bushes, as if to turn away intruders. The inhabitants of the house lived in isolation from the world, and from one another.

The only male occupant of the Herbert Street house was strong and handsome, yet he had remained closeted in an attic sanctuary for most of twelve years. Almost every evening he left the house to walk the streets of Salem and its rocky coast alone. Once a year he escaped altogether for a vacation in the outside world. He always returned to his attic to write somber tales and to burn much of what he wrote.

Another Salem site of special interest to the witches would have been the burial ground on Charter Street, final resting place of their persecuting judge. Next to the graveyard, without so much as a strip of grass or a bush between, stood an undistinguished white house. Its door, which opened directly into the street, was seldom still. Patients came to see the doctor who lived there. While they waited, they could contemplate the gravestones that stood directly under the doctor's office windows. Children came for lessons with one of the doctor's daughters. Matrons came to call on his wife. Yet this busy house was similar to the Herbert Street house in one respect. In an upstairs room lived another reclusive Salem citizen. She was a pretty young woman who painted pictures when she was sufficiently well. Most of the time she lay in a hammock, her fingers pressed to her aching head.

Assuming that the ghosts were vengeful, they must have enjoyed their flights over the entire city, for Salem was beginning to languish. Except for the infamous witch hunts, Salem's early history had been one of proud progress. The first colonists had sailed into Salem's harbor north of Boston just a few years after the Pilgrims had stepped off the *Mayflower* onto Plymouth Rock. They had fought the Indians and the elements

4

and farmed the rocky soil and fished along the rocky coast. Early in the 1700's they had begun to build tall ships to sail from Salem to ports in Europe and the Caribbean. During the Revolutionary War Salem's ships had fought the British on the high seas. When the war was over, the little city had entered its most glorious period. Salem ships had sailed to the Orient. One trader became the first American millionaire. He and other merchants built splendid mansions and filled them with treasures from around the world.

By 1837, however, Salem was already in a commercial decline. Ever larger ships were being built. Since the Salem harbor was too shallow to accommodate their deep hulls, they were docking at Boston piers. The signs of malaise were there for the ghosts to read: a closed mansion, an empty warehouse, a decaying dock. Proud Salem, once the tenth largest town in the United States, seemed destined to become just another sleepy fishing village.

Although Salem's population was stagnant, the population of the country as a whole was in the process of jumping from five million in 1800 to twenty-three million in 1850. The sixty-year-old nation had survived the Revolution and the War of 1812. Martin Van Buren was presiding as the eighth president of a country that was pushing constantly westward. Wagons had crossed the Rockies. Steamboats were chugging up and down the rivers. Railroad tracks were being laid.

During this period of commercial growth American men of letters, the arts, and ideas were becoming aware of themselves as Americans, rather than as transplanted

Europeans. Two New York authors, Washington Irving and James Fenimore Cooper, had already become famous both at home and abroad. The Hudson River school of artists was beginning to produce romantic landscapes. New religions and philosophies were being born. William Ellery Channing had introduced Unitarianism, a belief in the goodness of man as opposed to the belief in the depravity of man on which the Puritan faith was based. Henry Wadsworth Longfellow, Ralph Waldo Emerson, Henry David Thoreau, Oliver Wendell Holmes, and James Russell Lowell were all young men who were just beginning to make the contributions that would cause their age to be known as the "Flowering of New England." All lived in Boston or nearby Cambridge or Concord.

Meanwhile decaying old Salem, the delight of the witches, was sheltering a recluse on Herbert Street named Nathaniel Hawthorne. Destined to be released from solitude by his love for the invalid on Charter Street, Sophia Peabody, he would contribute the brightest blossoms to New England's intellectual bouquet.

1

The Recluse of Herbert Street

Nathaniel Hawthorne had been so long sequestered in his attic room that every glimpse of him must have been discussed in detail by Salem gossips. The details were most attractive, for he was tall, broad-shouldered, and slender. He had masses of dark, wavy hair; heavy eyebrows over large, deep blue eyes; a straight nose; a full, sensitive mouth; and a small cleft in his clean-shaven chin. The young women of Salem would ask one another how such a man could be so unsociable; he didn't even go to church. Older women would remind their daughters of other remote Hawthorne men—the two punitive judges and a brooding sea captain. Nathaniel Hawthorne was handsome—no one could deny that— but he was an unsuitable subject for the dreams of romantic young women.

◆◆◆

Hawthorne family history went back to sixteenth-century England. It was said that the family took its name from the Hawthorne tree, although later generations began to spell the name without the *w*. It was Nathaniel himself who chose to restore the *w*.

One of the first Hawthorne stories bears no trace of the bleakness that would become part of the family heritage. It concerns a simple but generous Englishman who owned an inn located just below Hawthorne Hill on a road between London and Oxford. Three times a beautiful woman came to the innkeeper in his dreams. Each time she told him that if he were to walk on London Bridge on a certain day, he would hear welcome news. He ignored the first two dreams, but when he woke after the third dream, he realized that it was the morning of the day he was to be in London. He saddled his best horse and rode to the city. He was walking on the bridge, wondering at his own foolishness, when a well-dressed but pompous-appearing man came and stood beside him and started a conversation. Within minutes the embarrassed innkeeper was telling about his dreams.

"Nonsense," said the well-dressed man. "I myself once dreamed that if I were to dig under the tree which tops Hawthorne Hill, I would find a treasure. But I am too wise to believe in dreams. Besides, I am far too busy to ride all over England looking for a place called Hawthorne Hill."

The stranger walked on and the innkeeper rushed

8

home, arriving late in the night. He unsaddled his weary horse, picked up a spade and a lantern, and climbed to the top of the hill behind his inn. Within a very short time he had unearthed a pot, which he carried back to the inn. By the light of the dying fire he saw that there was strange writing on the pot. He opened it and discovered that it was half filled with gold pieces.

The innkeeper hid the pot with the gold still in it in a heavy chest which he carefully locked. Then he went to bed. He could not sleep. Someone would surely steal his treasure. Or it may have been that the devil had put it there to tempt him. He told no one of his treasure. He was unable to sleep at night nor to keep his mind on his work by day.

Days went by. On the ninth day he had to go to a neighboring town. After conducting his business, he fortified himself with ale and rode home determined to share his secret with his family. It was late when he reached the inn and everyone had gone to bed, but he took the pot from the chest and placed it on the mantel.

Just as he was about to call his wife, he heard a knock at the door. The innkeeper was terrified. Surely the devil had come to claim his soul. He was unable to move. At last his wife got out of bed and came downstairs.

"Are you so rich that you can afford to turn away a paying guest?" she demanded as she unlocked and opened the door to two young priests from Oxford.

She called servants to arise to feed the priests. As they were sitting down to eat, one of the priests noticed the pot. The innkeeper, with a great feeling of relief, told his story. The priests examined the pot. It had been buried by the Romans centuries earlier, they said. The strange writing indicated that there was another pot buried under that pot.

Everyone, including the servants and the children, trudged to the top of Hawthorne Hill and there they found a second pot. It was just like the first but it bore no inscription. It was filled to the very brim with gold.

Back in the inn the priests asked who owned Hawthorne Hill.

"I do," said the innkeeper.

"Then you also own the treasure," said one of the priests.

Still the innkeeper was fearful until the priests at last convinced him that the vision of the beautiful young woman was sent by the Mother of God, who wished to reward the poor man for his kindness to strangers. The grateful man lived out his life in great happiness, providing for his sons and daughters, giving generous sums to the church and welcoming strangers to his inn.

◆◆◆

There was no trace of the kindly innkeeper in his descendant William Hathorne who immigrated to America soon after the Pilgrims and earned a few words in history for his vigor in persecuting Quakers. His son, Judge John Hathorne, earned a whole chapter in early American history for his pitiless persecution of "witches."

In the 1690's bored teen-age girls had been captivated by tales of ghosts and demons told to them by a servant from Barbados. Eventually the girls became virtually possessed by these stories and they began to writhe in pain and cry out in terror as they pointed to spirits that were invisible to others. Mystified, God-fearing adults blamed the devil working through witches. Three women were arrested and charged with witchcraft. The hysteria spread until more than a hundred women—as well as men and even a few children—had been arrested, jailed, and tried. Nineteen "witches" were sentenced to death and hanged on Gallows Hill just outside of Salem. The most vigorous of the judges to participate in the trials was said to be John Hathorne. One of the "witches" called down a curse upon him and his family so that when Hathorne fortunes began to decline, no one in Salem was surprised.

In spite of the curse the family lived quietly for several generations until "Bold Daniel" Hathorne earned brief fame as a daring sea captain during the Revolutionary War. One of his sons, Nathaniel, was also a sea captain. A moody man who loved solitude, Captain Nathaniel Hathorne was the father of the handsome young recluse on Herbert Street. Salemites noted the strange behavior of young Nathaniel and remembered the persecuting ancestors, the witch's curse, and the moody father. It's in his blood, they explained to one another.

The taste for solitude that Nathaniel Hawthorne inherited from his dour ancestors was fed by his mother. Elizabeth Manning was one of nine children of a blacksmith who had acquired two substantial businesses, a livery stable and a stagecoach line. He also owned a large tract of land in the wilderness of Maine. Manning women would never be invited to tea in the stately mansions of Salem but they were respectable. When Elizabeth Manning married Captain Nathaniel Hathorne, she raised herself on the rigid social ladder.

Captain Hathorne took his bride to live in a small house owned by his father's family, and there three children were born. The first two were named for their parents—Elizabeth, called Ebe, born in 1802, and Nathaniel, born on Independence Day, July 4, 1804. Soon after the birth of a third child, Louisa, in 1808, the captain died of yellow fever in a distant South American port.

When she received word of her husband's death, Madame Hathorne, still a young woman in her twenties, returned with her children to the Manning house on Herbert Street. Having been left almost nothing by her young husband, she was impoverished. She was also proud. If Hathorne relatives offered her financial assistance, she refused it, preferring to lean on her own family.

No one noticed anything peculiar about her behavior at first. She wore the somber black dresses that all new widows wore in those days. She shut herself away from the world, seldom leaving the house, taking most of her meals in her room. Her neighbors did not begin to whisper about her until it became obvious that she would never stop mourning. Her black dresses became rusty and outmoded but she continued to wear them. She spent more, rather than less, time in seclusion.

If the children received little attention from their

mother, they were not neglected, for they had plenty of substitute parents—their Manning grandparents and eight unmarried aunts and uncles. They were also taken to see their Hathorne relatives from time to time.

There was no hint of the recluse in the little boy. Nathaniel had a sunny disposition, a sturdy body, and a good mind. His sisters, as well as the Manning adults, adored him. He did not play much with other little boys but he had a number of animal companions—a monkey and many cats. When one of the cats died, the little boy buried him in the garden and printed the following verse on a slate which served as the cat's tombstone:

> Then, oh Thomas, rest in glory!
> Hallowed be thy silent grave,—
> Long thy name in Salem's story
> Shall live, and honor o'er it wave.

When he was nine years old, Nathaniel injured his foot while playing ball. For months he was confined to his home. He was taken from doctor to doctor in the hope of finding a cure. Interesting treatments were prescribed; for example, one called for the boy to thrust his injured foot from a downstairs window while someone threw a bucket of cold water on it from an upstairs window. When nothing seemed to help, his aunts and uncles began to look at him and shake their heads. The boy was permanently lame. Such a pity!

Nathaniel himself remained cheerful, since he had never liked school anyway. The schoolmaster came daily to hear his lessons but still he had endless hours to lie on the floor and read all the books in the Manning home. Of course he could not understand all of what he read, but he discovered stories and sentences that appealed to him. Shakespeare's *Richard III* contained one line that he entoned dramatically to himself and to anyone within earshot: "My Lord, stand back and let the coffin pass."

He also entertained his sisters—and himself—with stories about fantastic journeys he would take and marvelous adventures he would have. Each story ended with "And I'm never coming back again," uttered in a hushed and solemn tone.

Time at last cured his foot and restored him to robust health. During his lameness he had developed a love of books, appreciation of the dramatic and the morbid, and a taste for solitude. These would remain with him forever.

Soon after he was able to walk again, he and his sisters and their mother moved to Raymond, Maine, to a house that his Uncle Robert had built on the land acquired by Grandfather Manning. They lived alone and so Madame Hathorne was forced to take a more active interest in the development of her children. She might have become overprotective, but she did not. By his own report Nathaniel ran wild, hunting and fishing, skating and sledding. He tracked a big black bear for miles through the woods—without success—and went to school with local boys. It was a boy's paradise.

Uncle Robert traveled back and forth between Maine and Salem and gradually assumed the role of Nathaniel's guardian. He urged his ward to write well-constructed letters to him. Some of the letters still exist. They are filled with apologies: Nathaniel can think of nothing to say, his pen is scratchy, his paper is of poor quality.

In May 1819 the fourteen-year-old boy wrote that he had shot a partridge and a henhawk and caught eighteen large trout. "I am sorry you intend to send me to school again," he added, since mother can "hardly spare me."

Uncle Robert ignored his plea and on the day after his fifteenth birthday he was back in Salem attending Mr. Acher's school.

"I now go to a 5 dollar school," he wrote to his sister Louisa. "I that have been to a 10 dollar one. 'O Lucifer, son of the morning, how art thou fallen!' "

Grandfather Manning had died while Nathaniel was in Maine and several of his aunts and uncles had married and left home. The atmosphere on Herbert Street was less congenial to the teen-ager than it had been to the little boy. In letters to Maine he complained that he could not eat the guava jelly because Grandma was saving it until someone was sick. He had to eat the rotten oranges and save the good ones until they went bad. Grandma scolded him constantly.

Following is one of the letters he wrote to his mother:

Salem, Tuesday March 7*th* 1820

Dear Mother,

As we received no letter last week, we are in anxiety about your health . . . I have left school, and have begun to fit for College under Benjm L. Oliver, Lawyer. So you are in great danger of having one learned man in your family. Mr. Oliver thought I could enter College next commencement, but Uncle Robert is afraid I should have to study too hard. I get my lessons at home, and recite them to him at 7 oClock in the morning. I am extremely homesick. Aunt Mary is continually scolding at me. Grandmaam hardly ever speaks a pleasant word to me. If I ever attempt to speak a word in my defence, they cry out against my impudence. However I guess I can live through a year and a half more, and then I shall leave them. One good effect results from their eternal finding-fault. It gives me some employment in retaliating, and that keeps up my spirits. Mother I wish you would let Louisa board with Mrs. Dike if she comes up here to go to school. Then Aunt M. can't have her to domineer over. I hope, however, that I shall see none of you up here very soon. Shall you want me to be a Minister, Doctor or Lawyer? A Minister I will not be. I believe . . . Louisa has not written one letter to me. Well, I will not write to her till she does. Oh how I wish I was again with you, with nothing to do but go a gunning. But the happiest days of my life are gone. Why was I not a girl that I might have been pinned all my life to my Mother's apron. After I have got through college I will come down and learn Ebe Latin and Greek. I rove from one subject to another at a great rate.

> I remain
> your
> affectionate

and
dutiful
son,

and
most
obedient
and
most
humble
servant,

and
most
respectful
and
most
hearty
well-wisher
Nathaniel
Hathorne.

In another letter he told Ebe that he found his situation so dismal that he had taken to chewing tobacco "with all my might, which I think raises my spirits."

In addition to complaining and studying Nathaniel worked as a bookkeeper for his Uncle William. Working part time, he earned a dollar a week. He also attended concerts and the theater, read popular novels, and went boating and fishing—not an altogether unpleasant life! Louisa joined him in Salem in the summer of 1820 and they both took dancing lessons.

"Louisa seems to be quite full of her dancing acquirements. She is continually putting on very stately airs and making curtsies," scoffed her brother.

In August and September of 1820 he produced six issues of a hand-printed weekly newspaper called *The Spectator*. He had complained that Aunt Mary scolded him all the time; he used his paper to get even, printing the following ad:

"Wanted—A Husband not above seventy years of age. None need apply unless they can produce good recommendations, or are possessed of at least ten thousand dollars. The applicant is young, being under fifty years of age, and of great beauty. —Mary Manning, Spinstress."

Under "Domestic Intelligence" he published this notice: "The lady of Dr. Winthrop Brown, a son and Heir. Mrs. Hathorne's cat, Seven Kittens. We hear that both the above ladies are in a state of convalescence."

Under "Deaths": "We are sorry to be under the necessity of informing our readers that no deaths of importance have taken place, except that of the publisher of this Paper, who died of Starvation, owing to the slenderness of his patronage."

Even the "serious" articles—with such titles as "On Wealth," "On Solitude"—were humorous. The young editor also wrote poetry for his paper. In a letter to Louisa before she came to Salem, he had quoted some of his poems and then added, "I could vomit up a dozen pages more if I was a mind to." Four lines are enough to reveal that Nathaniel Hawthorne showed more promise as a letter-writer and as a journalist than as a poet:

Oh, do not bid me part from thee,
For I will leave thee never.
Although thou throw'st thy scorn on me,
Yet I will love forever.

During the summer of 1821 all three of Madame Hathorne's teen-agers were in Salem, but Nathaniel was writing to his mother, begging her to stay in Maine.

"You can never have as much comfort here as you now enjoy. You are now undisputed Mistress of your own House. Here you would have to submit to the authority of Miss Manning. If you remove to Salem, I shall have no Mother to return to during the College Vacations . . . Elizabeth is as anxious for you to stay as myself. She says she is contented to remain here for a short time, but greatly prefers Raymond."

In the same letter he told his mother that Uncle William had given Ebe a leghorn bonnet, "Of the moderate price of 15 dollars. It is so large that the most piercing eye cannot discover her beneath it."

———◆◆———

Although Hathorne boys were usually sent to Harvard, Uncle Robert Manning chose Bowdoin College, a tiny school in the wilderness of Maine, for his nephew. Bowdoin was much less expensive than Harvard, and Uncle Robert was not wealthy. Furthermore the school was convenient to Raymond, where Madame Hathorne was still living.

Both Uncle Robert and the tutor thought that Nathaniel was well prepared for college but the boy himself was terrified of rejection. Again and again during the stagecoach trip to the school the seventeen-year-old begged his uncle to be ready to leave town the minute the college officials turned him down. In spite of his nearly incapacitating state of nerves, however, he passed the entrance examination and was accepted for admittance within an hour of his arrival on campus.

Nathaniel was a mediocre student who did well in Latin and English and less well in every other subject. He excelled in collecting fines. Discipline was maintained by a system of fines and since he had a talent for breaking the rules, he soon distinguished himself, however ingloriously, as the student who was fined most frequently. He hated to present prepared speeches —an important part of the curriculum—and so he paid the fine. He also paid for failing to prepare themes, for not attending classes and prayers, for walking unnecessarily on the Sabbath, and for gambling. When he was caught playing cards, he was fined fifty cents and the president of the college wrote to his mother. The situation could have been worse if the president had known the full story, that the boys were playing for a bottle of wine rather than for mere money.

It was at Bowdoin that Nathaniel discovered the joys of friendship. There were two social groups at the small school. The best students, including Nathaniel's roommate and another young scholar named Henry Wadsworth Longfellow, who had entered college at age fourteen, belonged to the Peucinian Society. Nathaniel joined the fun-loving Atheneans. There, for the first time in his life, he became close to young men his own age. He came to prize his friendships with Horatio Bridge, Jonathan Cilley, and Franklin Pierce beyond all other Bowdoin experiences.

Bridge was a particularly supportive friend. During long walks in the woods or while they were picking blueberries or fishing, the two young men would contemplate their futures. Bridge probably knew that his friend had started a novel and he prophesied that Hawthorne would someday be a famous writer. Nathaniel certainly hoped he was right, as there was nothing else he wanted to be. He said that he could not be a clergyman and live by men's sins, a doctor and live by their illnesses, or a lawyer and live by their quarrels. He could go into business with one of his uncles but the idea was distasteful to him.

For a few pennies a fortune-teller who lived in a shack near the campus would see gold and beautiful women in their futures. Nathaniel looked forward to beautiful women but he was positive that he would never marry, so positive that he bet Cilley a barrel of the best Madeira wine that he would not be married on November 24, 1836. Each wrote out their wager and gave it to Bridge for safekeeping. If Nathaniel were not married in 1836, Cilley would have a barrel of wine delivered to him; if he were married, he would have the wine delivered to Cilley.

At the end of his third year Nathaniel began to get restless. He wrote Louisa one of his funniest surviving letters, telling her that he would get into serious trouble if he could not come home early. He begged her to write a letter that he could show to the president when he asked to be dismissed. She could write that their mother was ill, that some member of the family was dying or about to be married, that his elder sister needed to be escorted home from some distant place, or she could think up her own excuse, but she must write. If she didn't, he would be forced to forge a letter. Louisa's response is not known.

Back in Bowdoin for his senior year he was graduated eighteenth in a class of thirty-six, mediocre to the end of his college career. Better scholars were invited to give speeches at the commencement. Those who were not to be honored banded together in a club that met every week in a local tavern. There they had such good times that they became the envy of their more distinguished classmates.

When he left Bowdoin in 1825, Nathaniel Hawthorne seemed to be happy, sociable, and ready to face the future. No one could have predicted the transformation that took place as soon as he returned to Salem.

◆◆

I sat down by the wayside of life like a man under an enchantment, and a shrubbery sprang up around me, and the bushes grew to be saplings, and the saplings became trees, until no exit appeared possible, through the entangling depths of my obscurity.

Thus wrote Hawthorne about the twelve years following his graduation from Bowdoin. The boy who had

hiked and hunted in Maine, who had danced and published a humorous paper in Salem, and who had joined
frivolous organizations and tasted the joy of close
friendships at Bowdoin came home to the grim old
house on Herbert Street and locked himself in a dismal
upstairs chamber to brood, to study, to write—and to
burn most of what he wrote.

One by one the Mannings, through marriages and
deaths, had left the old house. Madame Hathorne, who
had returned from Maine while her son was in college,
was a seldom-seen shadow. She still wore the same
black widow's weeds. No one was invited to enter the
room where she spent her days alone. Meals were left
for her outside her closed door. Even her children seldom saw her.

Like an insidious disease, Madame Hathorne's isolation had infected her daughters. Ebe had shown great
promise as a child; she could read Shakespeare at the
age of six. She was bright and witty, interested in books
and politics. One would have expected her to attend
some of the frequent lectures in Salem, to have taken an
interest in what influential people were thinking and
doing. Had she mixed socially with her peers, she might
have married and thus relieved her mother of the financial burden of providing for her. Alternatively she
might have provided for herself with a teaching position. She did neither. Still in her early twenties she too
led a cloistered life, seldom leaving her room except to
go to the library or to walk alone by the sea.

Louisa was less clever and less withdrawn and might

have been a normal young woman had she lived in other surroundings. She did not have the strength to resist the influence of her mother and sister and so while she was still in her teens, she too withdrew from the outside world—though not to the same extent as her sister. With the help of a servant girl she kept the fires burning and the shabby furniture dusted. She delivered meals on trays to the hallways outside the closed doors of her mother, her sister, and her brother.

In contrast to the four sequestered Hathornes other Salemites were bustling about tending to their businesses and discussing the arts and the new religion. The seaport was declining in commercial importance but wealthy merchants were still entertaining their friends in their elegant mansions. One of America's first and finest architects was Samuel McIntire, a Salemite who had designed some of the mansions and had influenced many others. These houses, built in the Federal and Georgian styles, were graced with well-proportioned, sunny rooms; noble staircases; and beautifully carved woodwork. They were filled with furnishings and decorative objects brought to Salem from the Orient and Europe.

The people of Salem had always lived under the cloud of the Puritan religion, which emphasized the basic sinfulness of man. The devil was lurking in every corner; God was stern and demanding. The sun, however, was beginning to shine through the Puritan cloud. Respected clergymen were preaching a new faith. Man is basically good, they said, and he can depend on reason and conscience to earn him a place in heaven. Salemites listened to the preachers of the new gospel with approval and enthusiasm.

When he returned from Bowdoin, Nathaniel Hawthorne could have established himself within this lively group. A visit to one of his well-married Hathorne aunts, attendance at lectures or church services, even a few warm smiles to people he could have met on the street or in a store would have resulted in invitations to social gatherings. He made none of these overtures. Why? Some said it was pride. Certainly Ebe was aware of her intellectual superiority and may have felt disdain for what she considered to be the pretentions of some of her relatives and neighbors. Madame Hathorne's withdrawal may also have had its origins in pride. Forced to live on the charity of her own relatives, she may have wished to hide herself from her husband's more socially prestigious family. But the pride of the Hathorne women does not explain Nathaniel's behavior.

He had inherited a reticent nature from his father. That his reticence was extreme can be blamed on his mother's lack of warmth. It is impossible to imagine Madame Hathorne hugging or cuddling her children at any time after her husband's death. Nathaniel learned to depend on himself for entertainment. In spite of the camaraderie he enjoyed at Bowdoin, he never learned the art of social chitchat and all of his life he would find more pleasure in watching people than in conversing with them.

Furthermore his stories were to show that he was haunted by the gloomy faith of his Puritan ancestors, unlike his contemporaries who were talking about a loving God who smiled down on His obedient servants. If Nathaniel believed in God, He was the God of wrath, not reason.

Nathaniel may also have been lazy; certainly he was self-indulgent. He had been educated at the expense of his Manning uncles who might have expected him to help in their businesses. There is no record, however, that they ever chastised him. The Mannings seem to have been remarkably tolerant of one another's foibles.

So the young man returned to the unhealthy atmosphere of the Herbert Street house and succumbed to morbid retirement. Day after day, year after year, his companions were the books Ebe brought him from the Salem library, since he would not even go to the library himself. Every night near sundown he left his chamber for a long walk, usually along the shore. Very occasionally he visited someone in Salem. Once a year he went on a long trip, frequently with his uncle Sam Manning, who was a horse trader. Occasionally he went to Boston to meet Bridge.

Alone in his chamber he was reliving the lives of his ancestors and re-creating them with his pen. His first book-length manuscript was entitled *Seven Tales of My Native Land*. Ebe said that he showed the tales to her in 1825, that she liked them, and that some were about witches and some about pirates. That is all that is known of them. Nathaniel sent them from publisher to publisher until they landed on the desk of a Salem printer who said he wanted to distribute them and then did nothing. The author grew increasingly anxious as the handwritten manuscript sat month after month on a shelf in the printer's office. Finally in a fit of temper he went to the print shop, demanded the return of his manuscript, marched home with it, and threw it in the fire.

Years later Hawthorne wrote a tale he called "The Devil in Manuscript," in which the hero is a young author discouraged by his inability to sell his stories. He also burns his manuscripts. Watching his words burn, he sees his characters in the flames:

"There I see my lovers clasped in each other's arms. How pure the flame that bursts from their glowing hearts! And yonder the features of a villain writhing in the fire that shall torment him to eternity. My holy men, my pious and angelic women, stand like martyrs amid the flames, their mild eyes lifted heavenward."

While still in college the young author had begun work on a novel. It was probably *Fanshawe*, which he published anonymously and at his own expense in 1828. Most first novels are autobiographical; Hawthorne's was not. Instead it reads like an outline for a romance of the type that was popular at that time. Perhaps the author deliberately sat down to write a book that would make money. He failed.

The setting is a small college, like Bowdoin, and the surrounding countryside. The college president has a beautiful young ward whose father has been in Europe for many years. Just before the father is expected to return, the villain arrives. Believing the girl's father to be dead, he plans to marry her and thus gain control of her large fortune. He deceives the girl, telling her that he has been sent by her father. Then he lures her away from home and kidnaps her. As soon as the dastardly deed is discovered, the college president and two students, both of whom love her, set out to rescue the girl. One of the students is Fanshawe, whose health has been ruined by long hours of serious studying. He kills the villain and returns the girl to safety—and the arms of her father who has arrived at the appropriate dramatic moment. The heroine, realizing Fanshawe's undeclared love and her debt to him, offers to marry him. He, knowing that he cannot live long, refuses and dies. Eventually she marries the other student, a handsome, well-born, pleasant young man.

There are some moving scenes and colorful writing in *Fanshawe*, but the story is sketchy and the characters are flat. Hawthorne recognized the book's weaknesses soon after it was published. He then scurried around trying to retrieve and destroy every copy. Bridge burned his copy of the book at his friend's request. All but a few copies of *Fanshawe* went up in flames and the author erased the book from his mind, never again mentioning it.

Seven years of solitude passed slowly and with a sameness that made life seem to stand still. Nathaniel continued to write and finally his first tales were published. The 1832 edition of *The Token*, an anthology published annually by Samuel Goodrich in Boston, contained four stories by an anonymous author who was Nathaniel Hawthorne. They were "The Gentle Boy," "The Wives of the Dead," "Roger Malvin's Burial," and "My Kinsman, Major Molineaux." The author was paid thirty-five dollars for "The Gentle Boy," based on the experiences of the first American Hathorne, who had persecuted the Quakers. He received even less for some of his other stories and no recognition. Eight of his stories appeared in the 1835 edition of *New England Magazine* and nine in the 1837 *Token*. All were published anonymously or were identified as being "by the author of 'The Gentle Boy.'"

Publishers were asking for his stories and paying small sums for them. This little success made him wish for more. He seemed suddenly to become aware of his need to earn a living. Therefore when Samuel Goodrich offered him a job, he accepted it.

Early in 1836 he moved to Boston to edit *The American Magazine of Useful and Entertaining Knowledge*. This magazine, published monthly, contained a grand hodgepodge of long and short articles, poems, songs, and illustrations. The May issue, for example, contained articles about Alexander Hamilton, gold washing, homeless children in London, fashion in Hamburg, wild ducks, the nature of sleep, plus poems and an original song. Hawthorne's job called for no creativity and little talent. He had simply to compile the material—almost any material would do so long as there was enough of it to fill the pages—and prepare it for the printers.

Ebe, in Salem, was his assistant. That he felt contempt for his work is evident in the following advice he wrote to her:

". . . you may extract every thing good that you come across—provided always it be not too good; and even if it should be, perhaps it will not quite ruin the Magazine; my own selections being bad enough to satisfy anybody. . . . Finish your life of Hamilton. I wish you would write a biography of Jefferson to fill about 4 magazine pages and be ready in a month or six weeks. If you don't, I must, and it is not a subject that suits me. . . . In regard to ordinary biographical subject, my way is to take some old magazine and make an abstract—you can't think how easy it is."

He stayed in Boston for six months, during which time he and Ebe also prepared the copy for *Peter Parley's Universal History*, another project that made a great deal of money for Goodrich and almost nothing for the authors.

He lived frugally in a boardinghouse. He had to live frugally because, as he wrote Louisa in one letter soon after he arrived, "My present stock is precisely 34 cents. . . . All that I have spent in Boston, except for absolute necessaries, has been 9 cents on the first day I came. . . ."

While he was in Boston, his stories received their first published reviews. A notice in a London journal seemed to give him special pleasure. Basking in the sunshine of praise from abroad, he wrote Ebe that "my worshipful self is a very famous man in London."

In Boston he tasted the pleasures of mixing with men of the world and of participating in the life of a busy city, but he did not, perhaps he *could not*, stay. Whether it was the introverted Hawthorne who soon wearied of day-to-day contact with the outside world, or the creative Hawthorne who rebelled against using his pen to produce pedestrian prose, is not known.

Whatever the reason, he returned to Salem after only six months.

He was not happy at home either. His isolated chamber oppressed him. His stories and his life seemed worthless. He sank into a profound depression which he revealed in letters to Horatio Bridge in Maine. Bridge was frantic. Following are excerpts from two letters Bridge wrote a week apart in October 1836:

". . . You have the blues again. Don't give up to them for God's sake and your own, and mine and everybody's. Brighter days will come, and that within six months. . . ."

"Dear Hath,—I have just received your last, and do not like its tone at all. There is a kind of desperate coolness about it that seems dangerous. I fear that you are too good a subject for suicide, and that some day you will end your mortal woes on your own responsibility. However, I wish you to refrain till next Thursday, when I shall be in Boston, *Deo volente* [God willing]. Be sure and come and meet me in Boston."

Nathaniel Hawthorne and the world of literature owe much to that modest man, Horatio Bridge. His faith in his friend was never to waver. Not only did he encourage Nathaniel during their college days and intervene appropriately when he threatened suicide, he also risked his own money to bring his friend's genius to the attention of the reading public. When Bridge wrote of brighter days within six months, he had already taken steps to assure those brighter days. He had contacted Goodrich about printing a collection of Hawthorne's stories with the author's name prominently displayed on the title page. Goodrich was reluctant. Who could be sure that anyone would buy the book? Bridge therefore wrote a check for $250 as a guarantee against losses to the publisher. His only stipulation was that his sponsorship must remain secret. Imagine Bridge's dilemma when he learned that Hawthorne was so pathetically grateful to Goodrich for offering to publish his book that he intended to dedicate it to its publisher. Bridge wrote immediately advising his friend not to flatter Goodrich: ". . . there is no doubt in my mind of his selfishness in regard to your work and yourself."

And so *Twice-Told Tales* was published, containing eighteen of the thirty-six stories that had been printed up to that time. The author was no longer Mr. Anonymous, but one Nathaniel Hawthorne, who had by that time decided to include the *w* so that the pronunciation of his name would be clear.

To say that the book was an instant success would be an enormous exaggeration, but it was received kindly and there were enough buyers so that Goodrich did not cash Bridge's check. Years later when Hawthorne learned of his friend's generosity, he dedicated *The Snow Image* to his friend and thanked him in the preface to that collection of tales.

Hawthorne had not seen his classmate Henry Wadsworth Longfellow since graduation but he sent him a copy of *Twice-Told Tales*. Longfellow had yet to write "Listen my children and you shall hear . . ." and the other poems that were to make him famous, but he was already well respected as a professor at Harvard and as a man of letters. Upon receiving the book, he wrote a eulogistic review in the *North American Review*, a highly respected literary magazine. Hawthorne was delighted.

"Whether or no the public will agree to the praise which you bestow on me, there are at least five persons who think you the most sagacious critic on earth—viz. my mother and two sisters, my old maiden aunt, and finally, the sturdiest believer of the whole five, my own self," Hawthorne wrote after reading the review.

Still unaware of Bridge's help, Hawthorne went to Maine to spend a month with his friend. They swam and fished and looked at pretty girls. Hawthorne's two other close college friends were well launched in their political careers. Franklin Pierce had just been elected to the United States Senate and Jonathan Cilley was serving in the House of Representatives. When Bridge sent him the matrimonial wager made during their college days, Cilley wrote Hawthorne to ask, "Were you, on the fourteenth day of November last past . . . double or single? . . . Just now it would have pleased me more to have heard that you were about to become the author and father of a legitimate and well-begotten boy than book." The young congressman promised to send the barrel of wine and asked for a copy of Hawthorne's book that he might review it.

Even in his most solitary days Hawthorne had not

been immune to attractive women—there is evidence of several brief flirtations—but he was not prepared for the wiles of one Mary Silsbee, daughter of a senator from Salem. Had Hawthorne mixed in society, he might have heard of Miss Mary's reputation. She delighted in creating scenes. While in Washington she had written anonymous letters that resulted in the termination of her cousin's engagement to an English nobleman. There too she had met John Louis O'Sullivan, the editor of a magazine to which Hawthorne contributed. O'Sullivan no doubt told her about the handsome and mysterious author and when they were back in Salem brought Hawthorne to meet her. She was lovely and he was totally inexperienced with socially prominent young women. He began calling on her frequently and when she wrote asking for a secret meeting, he obliged. With appropriate blushes and pauses she suggested that O'Sullivan had tried to seduce her. The naive young man never doubted her. Rushing off like a knight to the rescue of the damsel in distress, he challenged O'Sullivan to a duel. Fortunately O'Sullivan was not so rash as to accept the challenge. Instead he wrote a letter of explanation that convinced Hawthorne of his friend's innocence and of the young lady's perfidy.

Dueling was frowned upon but practiced in those days. In 1804 Vice-President Aaron Burr had killed former Secretary of the Treasury Alexander Hamilton in the most famous duel in United States history. Just how close Nathaniel had come to killing or being killed was demonstrated to him a few weeks later when he received word of his friend Cilley's death. The young congressman had been challenged to a political duel, had been pressured into accepting the challenge, and had been shot and killed.

According to the calendar the author was thirty-two years old. Socially and emotionally, however, he was still a boy, his development having been arrested by his twelve years of seclusion. The publication of *Twice-Told Tales* had resulted in the gradual penetration of the "entangling depths of my obscurity" and Hawthorne had begun to take tentative steps into Salem's streets and drawing rooms.

2

The Invalid of Charter Street

While Nathaniel Hawthorne was slowly emerging from his third-floor refuge on Herbert Street, Sophia Amelia Peabody was becoming ever more anchored to her invalid's couch just five blocks away on Charter Street. Like the Hawthornes the Peabodys traced their ancestry to England. There had been a Peabody with King Arthur at the Round Table. In 1630 John Peabody and his two sons sailed to the New World. The family grew —Peabody families were large and healthy—and sometimes prospered. Sophia's father, Nathaniel Peabody, was a gentle man who lacked the assertiveness of some of his ancestors. He had been a contented Latin teacher at Phillips Academy in Andover, Massachusetts, when he met the forceful principal of the North Andover Academy for young ladies, Elizabeth Palmer.

Miss Palmer was excessively proud of her ancestors. Her grandfather had been a general in the Revolutionary War; her father, a friend of Paul Revere, had participated in the Boston Tea Party. Until she was eight, Elizabeth Palmer had lived in luxury. Then almost overnight the Palmer wealth had disappeared. The loss had to do with worthless paper money used to pay the Continental armies during the war, and the villainy, from the Palmer point of view, of John Hancock. General Palmer had borrowed money from Hancock to pay the men in his command, offering his estate in Massachusetts as security for the loan. When Hancock threatened to foreclose, General Palmer rushed to Connecticut to raise money by selling his land there. His return was delayed by floods and he arrived at his home just one half hour after the deadline, but Hancock's man had already taken possession. Eight-year-old Elizabeth never forgot the sight of her crippled grandmother being led from their home. At the age of sixteen Elizabeth began her career as a teacher, the only profession then open to genteel young women.

Elizabeth Palmer married Nathaniel Peabody in 1802. Eighteen months later their first child, Elizabeth Palmer Peabody, was born. The first years of the marriage were happy, but as time passed, Mrs. Peabody grew impatient with her unambitious husband. He was amusing and intelligent but he cared not one whit for wealth or prestige. She decided that she would prefer to be married to a fashionable city doctor than to a country schoolteacher. She scolded and fussed at him until he at last agreed to move to Cambridgeport and to attend medical lectures at Harvard. A second daughter, Mary, was born there in 1806. Unfortunately for Mrs. Peabody her husband discovered dentistry at Harvard. He had always been clever with his hands; he found he enjoyed making false teeth. So much for her dream of social distinction.

Although Mrs. Peabody took some pleasure in referring to her husband as "the doctor," her marriage had become oppressive to her when the family moved to Salem to establish Dr. Peabody's dental practice. There, on September 21, 1809, Sophia Amelia Peabody was born. Mrs. Peabody opened a school for young children in her home to supplement the doctor's meager income. She also continued to have babies at two-year intervals: Nathaniel in 1811, George in 1813, and Wellington in 1815.

Sophia was a sunny, spirited, sometimes naughty little girl. One of her first memories was of escaping from her yard at about age three.

"It was glorious," she wrote years later. "My steps were winged, and there seemed more room on every side than I had heretofore supposed the world contained. . . . What exquisite fun! I really think every child that is born ought to have the happiness of running away once in their lives at least. . . . I went up a street that gradually ascended till, at the summit, I believed I stood on the top of the earth. But alas! at that acme of success my joy ended, for there I confronted suddenly this beggar girl, the first ragged, begrimed human being I had ever seen. She seized my hand, and said 'Make me a curtsy.'

" '*No*' I replied, '*I will not!*' . . . How I got away and home again, I cannot tell. . . . I never told mamma anything about it. . . . A short time after the grievous encounter, my hobgoblin passed along, when I was standing at the door, and muttered threats, and frowned."

A year or so later Sophia was sent to visit her Grandmother Palmer. There she recalled playing with puppies. She tried to pick up one of them but her hands were small and the puppy was fat and squirmy. She dropped him on the pavement and he squealed loudly. Out rushed her Aunt Alice, a stately, handsome woman, who began to shake and scold Sophia. When the scene was over, the little girl went up to her grandmother's room and stood looking out of the window. There on the doorstep across the street sat a little beggar girl. Sophia thought she was the same child who had frightened her in Salem.

"I'll maul you!" said the beggar girl, with a scowling, spiteful face.

Sophia was terrified but she did not mention the incident to her grandmother, a stern old lady who always sent the child to bed in a remote part of the house at six o'clock, where she lay in terror of the street noises and the darkness and engulfed in loneliness until she at last fell asleep. The grandmother also insisted that she eat everything placed in front of her or go without food altogether.

Poor Sophia. In addition to a stern grandmother and temperamental Aunt Alice, there were also two younger aunts who delighted in torturing the child. Sometimes they opened a large book, which Sophia later assumed was the Bible, and commanded her to read. When she made mistakes, they laughed and shouted in derision. Once they asked her if she would like to see a beautiful garden. Of course she would. They led her to a doorway and pushed her through it. She fell down several steps into a pit of utter darkness. Another time they took her to a courtyard filled with turkeys and drove the turkeys "gobbling like so many fiends" toward her. "I expected to be devoured at once. My distress was immeasurable, and the enjoyment of the young ladies complete. Their mocking laughter made me feel ashamed of being miserable."

She recorded one other event from that horror-ridden visit, a large afternoon party given by Aunt Alice. "I was arrayed carefully for the occasion. Oh, shall I ever forget the torture of the little satin boots and of the pantalettes, to which I was doomed? besides a general sensation of utter discomfort and bondage!" She was passed around among the ladies at the party "like a toy, as one of the entertainments, I suppose. But being in great bodily pain from my dress, as soon as I was released from their caresses, I escaped, and darted up the grand staircase as far as I could go, and fled into a room where I thought I should be undisturbed. There I untied the cruel strings that fastened the pantalettes round my ankles . . . and managed to pull them wholly off . . . glad to be released so far, I gayly returned to the drawing-room. Alas for it! The Lady Alice was immediately down upon me, like a broadwinged vulture on a most innocent dove. . . . She swooped me up, and consigned me to a servant to be put to bed in the middle of the afternoon."

An uncle eventually took her home to her family. Her mother, or perhaps her sister Elizabeth, taught her to read. Soon after she could read English, Dr. Peabody began to teach her Latin. The family enjoyed a few years of relative ease after the War of 1812. Salem merchants were prospering and were anxious to have their teeth cared for properly, so Salem's dentist also prospered. Mrs. Peabody gave up her school and had time to socialize with her neighbors.

By 1819, however, the nation, Salem, and hence Salem's dentist, were in a state of financial depression. It was during this low time that a seventh child, Catherine, was born, to live only a few weeks. Mrs. Peabody had endured this pregnancy with ill will, resenting her husband's inability to provide for her financially or socially and feeling already overburdened with six children. Nevertheless Catherine's death was a calamity for the whole family, so acute was Mrs. Peabody's sense of guilt. She had not welcomed the new baby so God had punished her. Her remorse was to have a long-lasting effect on the family, and especially on her youngest living daughter, Sophia.

In the meantime hard times had also come upon Mrs. Peabody's dearest friend, Mrs. Richard Cleveland, and she had moved to Lancaster, Massachusetts, to establish a boys' school. Mrs. Cleveland convinced Mrs. Peabody to move her family to a farmhouse nearby to establish a girls' school. Soon after the first pupils were gathered together, Mrs. Peabody turned her new school over to

Elizabeth, who at the age of sixteen began her lifelong career as a distinguished educator. Elizabeth's assistant was her fourteen-year-old sister Mary. Sophia, a merry, mischievous eleven-year-old in spite of family misfortunes, was a pupil in her sisters' school. It was the only school she ever attended.

During the summer of 1822 Sophia stood in the doorway between childhood and young womanhood. She ran through fields and waded in streams—and argued with Mary. According to one letter to Elizabeth, who was visiting in Cambridge and Boston, she and Mary went down to the river determined to cross it even "if we had to go over our heads in the attempt but as fortune would have it we had a very refreshing '*paddle*' and went off proud of our victory although we quarrelled because I said Mary was frightened and that I was not."

They made up after that quarrel and were soon on to another. Sophia complained that Elizabeth never wrote to her. She read the letters that Mary received, "that is those she will let me read which are *very few*." In the same letter she said she would take Elizabeth's advice about kissing games. "You know yourself that I detest them." Kissing games with the boys from Mrs. Cleveland's school seem to have been part of the regular, if unauthorized, entertainment.

Sophia's popularity with the boys got her into trouble, which she related proudly to Elizabeth. She had gone into the woods alone with one of the students, Frank Dana. She wouldn't have gone, she explained, except that she thought Mary was right behind her.

Mary was not and Mrs. Cleveland, when she found out about it, was upset and scolded Sophia.

"Do *you* think it is wrong for both of us to walk with Frank Dana?" Sophia asked Elizabeth.

Sophia was exuberant, pretty, and popular. Mary was reserved and plain and Sophia complained that she wrote all the news in her "plain matter of fact sort of way." If given a chance Sophia could tell the same news "in a much more elevated and witty style." Furthermore Mary criticized Sophia's sentences "as if she were my governess . . . my ears are regaled with *Pooh! Pooh!* you fool! how silly! and all such encouraging speeches."

Frivolity was only a part of Sophia's nature; she was also bright and eager to learn and she devoted long hours every day to sating her thirst for knowledge.

"I am studying Fergusons Astronomy—surely there is nothing so *interesting,* so *sublime* or so *useful* as astronomy. . . . I am likewise studying Chemistry which I find exceedingly interesting. . . . I study a lesson in Latin every . . . morning and recite it to Father at noon . . . Saturday composition . . . Wednesday arithmetic. . . . I [should] be perfectly happy if I could go to *college* [and work in a Chemistry lab]. What advantages *gentlemen* have! How they all ought to *shine* when they have so many ways to learn!"

College, of course, was out of the question for the simple reason that there was at that time no college anywhere in the United States open to women. Sophia was determined to be educated, however, and so she turned to her sister Elizabeth for guidance. "I hope that you will write me a long letter . . . a very long one full of good advice and I will follow it to the utmost extent of my powers," she wrote on the front of the letter to Elizabeth about her studies.

While still in her teens Elizabeth had stepped into the position of family manager. Dr. Peabody had become a leaf in the stream, floating along with his family, causing scarcely a ripple. Mrs. Peabody, feeling herself to be overburdened by her responsibilities, needed a strong arm to lean on and she turned to her oldest child. Mrs. Peabody had been happy while she was pregnant with Elizabeth and during the first few years of the child's life, and therefore Elizabeth was her strongest child. That at least was the mother's conviction. Whatever the reason, Elizabeth was energetic, forceful, and positive. She liked to give advice and she adored her pretty little sister. When she received Sophia's letter, she declined an invitation to a dinner party and devoted an evening to producing seven closely written pages of pompous advice. Following are a few typical sentences from that letter:

"I cannot think that I was more reflective at twelve years old than *you* are; at least, I *am sure*, I was not more *capable* of it, therefore I write to you not as a *child* to be advised—but as one who like myself is *seriously* engaged in a *serious* thing, and looks abroad with anxiety to every source of knowledge . . . cultivating the intellectual powers is a moral duty. . . . I hope—oh *I hope from my inmost heart*, . . . that the studies in

which you are now engaged will be pursued with un-
remitted industry—because they will strengthen your
mind—they will form the best *discipline* for it,—they will
give power to your faculties, they will strengthen your
powers of reasoning and judging, and you will be better
able to act in every situation of difficulty with energy
and firmness. Let your recreations be innocent and
pure. A garden of flowers will afford amusement. . . . In
gazing at nature, you should endeavor to observe with
accuracy. . . . I wish you now to read only those poets
with whom no one has found fault and which are perfectly moral. . . . When I write next I will take up two
more points—one—*religious habits* . . . and then point
out to you, as well as I am able, how you are to regulate
your feelings when reading that book of all others the
most varied, the most agitating, the most interesting—
the book of human nature."

That letter was followed by others just as long, just as
pedantic. And it was not only Sophia who was bom-
barded with Elizabeth's advice. Several years later at the
end of the school year in 1825 she wrote letters to all her
students "telling them in black and white what I thought
of their characters—both in school and out of school.
This led me to some disagreeable truths. . . ."

Surprisingly Sophia appeared to welcome her sister's
advice. Observing a garden had to have been tame entertainment compared to wading or kissing games but
there is no indication that she ever said so.

When school opened again in the fall, thirteen-year-
old Sophia was no longer a student but a teacher. Eliza-

beth remained in Boston and then accepted a job as governess to the younger children in a large, wealthy family in Maine. Mary became head teacher in the Lancaster girls' school and Sophia her assistant.

The following year the family moved back to Salem. Sophia's first letters to Elizabeth are filled with gossip and fun. One night she and Mary and several young cousins and friends went for a long walk by moonlight. It was eleven o'clock when they got home and Dr. and Mrs. Peabody had retired, leaving a lamp burning for their daughters. They were not upset but Elizabeth was and she wrote to reprimand Sophia for her indiscretion.

"But, Elizabeth," replied Sophia, "there was *such* a moon that it was almost impossible to resist the temptation."

In Salem Sophia continued her studies. She longed for the day when the boys would begin to learn Greek so that she could study with them. Even the education-oriented Peabodys would not consider hiring a Greek tutor for a girl, although Elizabeth had studied Greek in Boston with Ralph Waldo Emerson, then an eighteen-year-old unknown. Art was a more suitable subject for a young girl, and Sophia took drawing lessons.

Writing from Maine, Elizabeth suggested that Sophia join her, as the family for whom she was working needed a second teacher.

"I was surprised, glad, sorry, astonished, [and] delighted, to think that you had thought of my going to Hallowell so soon," responded Sophia. "I should be delighted to come, on account of assisting you, living with you, and the *society*, and *my improvement*, but what think you that the young ladies will say to see such a pigmy as *I* come to teach them! Oh, that I could shoot up a *yard* both in *acquirements* and *height* before next December! . . . Don't you think that Mary had better come the first year and let me be older? She wants to go *very much* and I should think it would be the best way. I guess it will be the first instance of a person's going into a school at *fourteen*. . . . I will leave it *entirely* to your judgement *to go* or *not* to go . . . though *I* think myself too small both ways."

Mary did go to Maine and was there until the two young women returned to open a school in Boston.

It was during her early teen-age years that Sophia began to have headaches. As they grew increasingly frequent and persistent, the family began to seek causes and cures. Mrs. Peabody, of course, said they were caused by her own unhappy condition before and after Sophia's birth. Dr. Peabody said that she had been a healthy baby until she began to cut her first teeth; he thought that the drugs he had prescribed then may have caused the headaches years later. They seem to have been sinus headaches and they may have been allergy related.

Every then-known treatment was tried to relieve her pain: hypnosis, arsenic, morphine, other drugs, a diet of white bread and water. Mary sent her a batch of leeches, little flatworms that were placed on the painful area to suck out blood. Sophia thanked Mary profusely:

. . .

"Those incomparable, lovely, delicate, gentle, tender, considerate, generous, fine, disinterested, excellent, dear, elegant, knowing, graceful, active, lovely, animated, beautiful *leeches* have done me a world of good. I have done things with this head of mine . . . which in former times would have cracked every brain. . . . I have been to Church *all day*—have laughed, run, read, written as much, if not more than formerly, and yet I remain comparatively free from pain."

The leech improvement did not last long. Leaving home was the only treatment that seemed to have any real effect on her health. Although Mrs. Peabody was reluctant to let her daughter out of her sight, Dr. Peabody took Sophia to visit his family in New Hampshire in 1824. It was a two-day trip by carriage over rough roads "yet I did not feel fatigued in the smallest degree, and as I had a great desire to go to Uncle Frank's I went—It was a mile from G[randfather]s and I had to mount a hill compared to w[hic]h Gallow's [sic] Hill is a *mole* hill—and to descend which I was obliged to support myself by bushes and trees or I should have been precipitated into the bright rolling river. . . ."

She continued to describe all of her adventures and then wrote, "And mind, I did not feel tired or fatigued after riding 120 miles besides climbing mountains—till I had got home."

A year later she went to visit friends and wrote Elizabeth the following: "I felt so much better than I have *since I can remember. . . .* You have no idea how strangely it felt to be *almost entirely* free from headache."

Sophia lived before the age of modern psychology; religion was the source of most insights into the mind. "Honor thy father and thy mother" was one of the Ten Commandments, hence she never questioned the quality or motives of her mother's love. Mrs. Peabody was a complicated woman whose husband was a disappointment and whose sons were normal, noisy boys. Her elder daughters had made lives for themselves quite apart from her, although she demanded from them a certain amount of pity. For example she wrote the following to Mary:

"Such was the situation into which the revolution and other circumstances plunged our family, that I was deprived of nearly all the advantages of that kind of parental care, which forms the heart, cherishes the good and erases the evil which circumstances implanted there. My disposition requires the gentle influence of tenderness and encouragement and dreadful have been the trials and struggles the want of that influence subjected me to."

She was determined to receive tenderness from Sophia and she took advantage of the girl's headaches to hold her close. Furthermore she had religion to reinforce her. Mrs. Peabody believed, and she taught Sophia to believe, that cheerful suffering would be pleasing to God. She would surely die while still a young woman but she would be rewarded in heaven.

Not all of the blame can be placed on the mother. Sophia docilely accepted, even enjoyed, her role as the saintly invalid. She could not compete with Elizabeth, who earned admiration for her clever mind, unlimited energy, and forceful personality, or with Mary, but she could earn admiration as a romantic martyr to ill health. Her role was to be the cheerful friend and devoted daughter who spread sweetness and light wherever she went. What prevented Sophia from being absolutely odious was her sense of humor which was apt to bubble forth even as she was being most melodramatic.

Mary, who always held herself a little apart from her mother and sisters, was said to have been a gifted teacher. She had a full share of the Peabody intelligence, a beautiful singing voice, and a quiet sense of humor. She probably recognized Sophia's saintliness as a pose and longed for the spirited little sister who had enjoyed a good quarrel.

In spite of her headaches Sophia led a reasonably active life. She helped her brothers with their studies and tried to spur them on to a more active interest in intellectual achievement. She continued her own studies and her art lessons. Her two greatest pleasures were her friends and her art. She had a gift for friendship and the same letters in which she described her ill health in great detail often reported visits to and from half a dozen different people.

In 1827 she went to visit an aunt in Brattleboro, Vermont. Unfortunately Sophia never learned to keep quiet about the pleasures she was enjoying when she was away from home. The more she wrote about horseback riding and parties, the more apt Mrs. Peabody would be to insist that she come home. Sophia had not been in Vermont long when she received a letter from her mother reminding her of her ill health and telling her that it was her duty to return home to her studies and to helping the boys with theirs. "Besides, I must acknowledge, that the kind and cheering tones of your voice and your mirth-inspiring laugh, and affectionate smile would be cordial to me. . . . The warm weather oppresses me and I have less strength to bear it than formerly." Self-pitying Mrs. Peabody continued her letter with a warning that excitement was not good for Sophia's head. "You enjoy too fervently for your strength. Come home now and live awhile upon the past."

Sophia went home but she did not have to "live on the past" for long. By mid-winter she was looking forward to living in Boston, an exciting place in the 1820's. While Salem was declining in importance as a port city, Boston was thriving. It was also a center for religious and cultural activity. Elizabeth had come to idolize William Ellery Channing, a distinguished clergyman who was one of the leaders in the movement away from the hellfire and damnation theology of the Puritans. Dr. Channing, nearing fifty and happily married, had not the slightest romantic interest in young Elizabeth but he admired her mind and invited her to his home where she met many of the leading intellectuals of the time. Both Mary and Elizabeth, whose new Boston school was prospering, had a wide circle of interesting friends who would become Sophia's friends too.

For the first time in many years the whole Peabody family was together in Boston, although Dr. Peabody returned to Salem four days every month to take care of his patients there. He had just written a book entitled *The Art of Preserving Teeth* in which he suggested that decaying teeth might be filled rather than extracted.

In Boston Sophia began to think of a future means of earning her own livelihood. The obvious career—indeed the only career open to most women—was teaching. Although she loved children and they loved her, she did not enjoy teaching. Furthermore she lacked the physical stamina necessary for regular work in a classroom. Her interest was in art and since wealthy Bostonians were often willing to pay respectable fees for copies of popular paintings, Sophia hoped that she could learn to become a competent copier and thus earn her way with her paintbrush. Family manager Elizabeth therefore set about obtaining the best art instruction possible for her sister. Francis Graeter was her first instructor. He was followed by an already well-known landscape artist named Thomas Doughty. Somehow Elizabeth persuaded Doughty to set up his easel in Sophia's room so that she could watch him paint without leaving her invalid's couch. He came for the first time in June 1830 and Sophia reported in her journal that he did not look a "bit like a genius—not a bit." A week later he told his student that her work was very well done, much better than he had expected.

Doughty came to her but she went to Chester Hard-ing, a portrait painter who asked Sophia to come to his studio to sit for him. She insisted that she "had no features" but she went because she could learn about portraits while she was being painted.

She was not a beautiful young woman but she was small and graceful. She had light brown hair and gray eyes. It was her smile that seems to have set her apart from hundreds of merely pretty young women. Years later in *The Marble Faun* Nathaniel Hawthorne was to describe his heroine, who obviously looked like Sophia Peabody, in these words:

"She was pretty at all times, in our native New England style, with her light-brown ringlets, her delicately tinged but healthful cheek, her sensitive, intelligent, yet most feminine and kindly face. But, every few moments, this pretty and girlish face grew beautiful and striking, as some inward thought and feeling brightened, rose to the surface, and then, as it were, passed out of sight again."

Young Harvard students also thought her attractive and most days several of them would come calling upon her. They came in vain, for Sophia, like many women before and after her, was falling in love with her doctor. Her secret affection was recorded in her journal. It went unnoticed by her family and friends, who would have considered the alliance to be most unsuitable. The doctor was none other than the younger brother of William Ellery Channing, the clergyman whom Elizabeth found so admirable. Dr. Walter Channing was twenty-three years older than Sophia, a widower and a father. The first professor of obstetrics at Harvard and the dean of Harvard Medical School, he was among the first to use ether to relieve the pain of childbirth. He was also a poet and essayist.

In May of 1830 Sophia wrote, "I received a sweet smile and kind shake from dear Dr. Walter C. which revived me wonderfully." A few weeks later she wrote, "After church Mr. Alcott was married to Miss May and Dr. Walter who was there, thought we had better stay, and we did." Louisa May Alcott, who was to become the famous author of *Little Women*, was born to the marriage that Sophia attended. Her younger sister Beth, whose death is one of the most poignant scenes in the novel, was named after Elizabeth Peabody. "Dear Dr. Walter came home with us and staid till nine—as agreeable every moment of the four hours as it was possible for man to be."

One Sunday in June Sophia accepted Dr. Walter's invitation to go home with him. He read some of his pieces "in a tone that rang through my depths." When he returned her to her own home, he examined her aching head and wanted to "probe" it but she felt "altogether too sick and tired and nervous to be touched in any way." The following Sunday he came after church "for a few minutes" and stayed two hours. In the meantime she copied some of his poems and read an article he had written.

In August twenty-two-year-old Sophia packed her palette and left home. Perhaps it was her hope of becoming the second Mrs. Walter Channing that gave her the courage to make a break with her mother. Mrs. Peabody could not have let her go willingly but both she and Dr. Peabody took Sophia to Dedham, a small town outside of Boston. After they had dined with friends, they left her in a rooming house.

"Here I am in the holy country, alone with the trees and birds—my first retreat into solitude." There, established in a room with extensive views, she hoped to earn her way copying oil paintings. One of her windows provided a "dear little peep" of Havenwood through the trees. Havenwood was the home of one of her dearest friends, Lydia, the recent bride of Sam Haven. She had little solitude, her days being filled with walks with Lydia and dinners at Havenwood. Although her head ached for days after her arrival, she gradually began to feel better and she was soon sketching and painting, taking long walks, climbing rocks, and riding a horse. Dr. Walter wrote to her.

She made a valiant effort to support herself but she was not totally successful. In October she received a letter from her father addressed as follows: "Lady Sophia Peabody, Princess of Dedham, Now residing on her estate in the vicinity of Havenwood where she is a frequent Visitor. Intimate acquaintance of Queen Lydia an exceedingly interesting Sovereign." After that whimsical address the letter began, "Dear Sophia, No one seems to be at leisure to write to you so I substitute myself having nothing to say." What he did say was that he didn't have the money to pay her landlady just then, but he expected to have it soon.

Winter came and Sophia had to return to Boston. Her

sadness at her inability to live independently was probably tempered by her joy at seeing Doctor Walter again. The doctor was certainly attentive to Sophia, but who can tell if he ever saw her as anything more than a pretty girl and an interesting patient? He was one of the few who suspected that her illness was at least partly psychosomatic. In her journal Sophia wrote that one doctor had said that she would never be relieved of her headaches until death. "Dr. Shattuck was right when he so decidedly declared I never should be relieved 'till I heard the music of the sphere'—in other words till I had put off corruption."

On the very same day, Dr. Walter counted her pulse and looked at her tongue and said they were both normal. "'I find no fault in you,' he said, 'but you have grown thinner. Take Quassis—it is bitter—but bitters are sweets to you.' I did not take his meaning but supposed it agreeable." It is difficult to imagine Sophia being so dense. Surely "bitters are sweets to you" meant simply that he thought she was enjoying her poor health.

Three days later Sophia discovered that the second Mrs. Walter Channing would be one Elizabeth Wainwright. Several days after Sophia heard the news, Dr. Walter called on her.

"I knew it was he and I opened to him with a leaping sensation—which I could not account for—but the moment I met his brilliant, joyous eyes—and he took both my hands in the warmest manner, I saw just how unreserved he felt and I immediately was at ease. *He told me about it*—with a simplicity and delight which charmed me renewedly. The universe on the bridge of my nose which I have carried there all day seemed to be lifted up the while he was here—and when he went, he took off his glove and in such a sweet way—shook my hand—that not a word could I say. . . . When he had gone—the universe returned and I had to lie down upon the bed till dinner."

One other famous artist was to instruct Sophia. He was Washington Allston. After Harvard, Allston went abroad for seventeen years, returning to Boston with a well-established reputation as an artist. He brought with him a huge, nearly completed canvas which was to be his masterpiece and a rival to the old masters. Ten Bostonians each gave one thousand dollars to buy the painting in advance. Years passed while Allston continued to paint on the masterpiece he allowed no one to see. Twenty-five years passed and still he was painting on that one picture with time out to paint "less important" works from time to time. After his death his patrons gathered to unveil the work that had been almost completed twenty-five years earlier. Their silent awe and expectation turned to horror as a monstrous work was revealed. Still unfinished, it had been painted over and over as the artist tried unsuccessfully to translate his vision to canvas.

The mystery painting was still in progress when Allston condescended to call on Miss Sophia Peabody. He took one of her pictures in his famous hands and examined it carefully.

"I have no fault to find with it," he said at last. "I am very much surprised at it, for it is superior to what I expected."

The next Peabody picture he looked at did not please him. It was a copy of a French painting and Allston told the young artist that she should paint from nature, not copy other paintings. He did, however, give her permission to copy his own latest work and he also suggested that she visit his nephew and protégé, a boy of sixteen, who would repeat Allston's lessons for her benefit.

Once Sophia began to copy Allston's painting, she reported in her journal that the experience was "almost intoxicating." Of course she was sick—she was always sick—but she painted with "singing delight." "Why am I so privileged as to be able to exercise this divinest art?" she asked her journal.

As word of Sophia's success as a copyist spread, she found herself under ever greater pressure to produce. She wanted to paint something original as Allston had suggested but Elizabeth was continually borrowing pictures for her to copy and selling the copies before they were even begun. The young artist had no time to create.

Then Elizabeth dreamed up a truly monumental job for her sister. Elizabeth decided to retell the Greek myths for publication in a book to be illustrated by Sophia. Sophia should have refused—she was already overburdened with orders for copies and she knew absolutely nothing about lithography, a method of printing from engravings made on stone—but Sophia never said

no to Elizabeth. She tried to learn about lithography
from the man Elizabeth sent to instruct her. Nothing
went well. Elizabeth sent sketches of statues she wanted
reproduced in the book but they were almost useless to
the artist. The stones were heavy and dirty. She had
great difficulty transferring her own sketches to the
stones and when they were finished and shipped off to
the printer, the proofs were disappointing.

The pressure was too much for Sophia. Her already
poor health deteriorated further. Her family decided
that she was near death. New Englanders had great
faith in the restorative powers of sunny lands and a trip
was the usual prescription for the terminally ill. Sophia
would have to go south. But how could that be ar-
ranged? The family was once again in financial trouble. Mary and Elizabeth had taken a partner into their
school, as a result of which it failed. The Peabody boys
had been expelled from Harvard after running up debts
that had somehow to be paid. There simply was no
money for a trip. As in the past, however, Elizabeth
found a way. A wealthy coffee planter in Cuba needed a
governess for his children. Elizabeth decided that Mary
could fill the position and take Sophia with her to be a
guest of the household. It made no difference that Mary
did not wish to go. Her reason was a secret: she was in
love with Horace Mann, who was still mourning for his
first wife.

Two young women could not go alone on such a voyage, but the problem of finding an escort for them was
also surmounted. A friend sent Mary word of a Negro

slave who had brought two children to Boston where they were to be educated. She was a nurse, the wife of the overseer of a plantation, spoke both Spanish and English, and had been back and forth several times. She would escort the young ladies.

On December 4, 1833, Mary, Sophia, and the servant set sail on the *New Castle*, a two-masted ship with square sails. The slave had not previously met the two young women and it was an indication of things to come when she had to ask which of them was the invalid. While the ship was still in harbor, Sophia began to delight in the voyage and her fellow passengers—especially a man whose name was crossed out seven times in her first letter home. He had "an exhaustless fund of anecdote" and was "so attentive and ingenious in devices to make our time pass agreeably that he quite annihilates time and space." Mary, on the other hand, was grieving and spent her time on shipboard reading and making dozens of pin cushions.

A month after leaving home they were at La Recompensa, the estate of Dr. Morrell, a coffee planter and medical doctor; his wife; teen-age daughter; and two young sons. Communications between Cuba and Massachusetts were slow and irregular but Sophia wrote almost every day. Whenever she had an opportunity, she gathered her letters together and sent them off with a passenger on a ship bound for Boston. They were delivered to Elizabeth, who sent them on to Salem where Dr. and Mrs. Peabody were once again living. The letters were passed among family and friends and then bound into three volumes which came to be known as the *Cuba Journals*.

Sophia saw with an artist's eye and her descriptions of life on the exotic island were vivid, often amusing:

"Don Antonio . . . looks exactly like a feather bed with his head, arms and legs tied off."

"This tropical heat is nothing less than delicious. . . . It is exactly like being in a perfumed bath all the time."

"A dawn ride. It was an emerald-set-in-pearl morning."

A black cloud is like "a heavy frown on the brow of night."

Since Mrs. Peabody was especially interested in gardening, Sophia often described the plant life in Cuba and sketched leaves and flowers.

Dr. Morrell's estate turned out to be a healthy environment for Sophia. Although her headaches continued, she began to feel energetic. Part of this was due, no doubt, to the fact that she was away from home and mother. She was also eating well. Little was known about nutrition and Sophia's invalid diet in Massachusetts had been deficient in vitamins and protein. Meals in Cuba were rich in fruit and meats. Exercise also helped Sophia attain new levels of energy. She was given a horse to ride and almost every morning she and Eduardo Morrell, age nine, rose before sunrise, ate oranges left in a bowl in the main hall for them, and went for a ride. One of Sophia's great delights was in picking more oranges from the

trees and eating them as she rode. After riding about
the estate for several hours they returned to the house
where Sophia took a rest. Breakfast was served late in
the morning and consisted of meat, eggs, and fruit.
Dinner was served in the late afternoon and then Sophia
often went riding again. Tea was served about nine
o'clock in the evening.

Friends from neighboring estates came to visit the
Morrells almost every day, often arriving for breakfast
and staying for dinner and tea. Mary was kept busy
teaching Eduardo and his little brother Carlito. She also
read aloud to Mrs. Morrell. Sophia had no responsibilities, but she often entertained the children. She also
drew pictures of the Morrell family, the slaves of the
house, the plantation, and the most frequent visitors,
among whom were two young brothers, Fernando and
Manuel. Fernando was "perfectly inspired" at the piano
and much time was spent with music and dancing.
Toward the end of the summer in Cuba Sophia wrote
the following in a letter to her mother:

"What think you dearest mother I did this evening?
You will never imagine in the world. I *waltzed*!! and
though I was very dizzy the first time, I whirled round
without discomfort before I gave up!"

The next day she wrote that she thought waltzing
was good for her. On the following day she went for a
moonlight walk with Mary, Fernando, and others. They
walked for miles and miles.

. . .

"I sat down in a rocking chair with considerable *gusto* when I got home but was neither speechless nor helpless and Fernando did not go away till quarter of eleven and yet I felt bright and very well."

Another evening they played Puss in the Corner by moonlight.

"Do not be alarmed, dearest Mother—I did not run very hard."

Imagine Mrs. Peabody's concern when she received these letters. Her darling Sophia was showing signs of health and independence. She wrote immediately to warn her daughter about the dangers of exercise. Sophia responded dutifully; she had only waltzed as an experiment to see if it would clear her head and she would never try it again. She also reassured her mother of her love of home.

"My life in Cuba will always be to me like a superb pageant. . . . I love any old poplar tree in New England better than any productions peculiar to this foreign Paradise."

Sophia and Mary were teaching English to Manuel while he was teaching Spanish to them. Mary delighted in teaching him ugly words like *squawk*. The Morrell daughter added *brats* to his vocabulary so that one of the first English phrases he learned, and one which he repeated over and over, was "Brats squawk."

Sophia's Spanish improved unevenly. Manuel asked her if she liked oranges better than pineapples. She replied that the pineapples grown on the estate had been so poor that year that they had been fed to the *colchón*. What animal is that? asked Manuel, always polite and understandably confused, for *colchón* means *mattress*; *cochino* is the word for hogs.

Lancaster history repeated itself in Cuba. Merry Sophia was again indiscreet, and again Mrs. Cleveland, that dear friend of Mrs. Peabody, felt it her duty to see that she was reprimanded. Mr. Cleveland was, at the time of their arrival, American consul in Havana and the Peabody girls had stayed in his home before going on to La Recompensa. They had seen Mrs. Cleveland on several other occasions. When the old gossip returned to Salem, she took with her a choice story about Sophia and James Burroughs, the man who had been so delightful on board the ship and whose name had been crossed out seven times in one letter. He had accompanied Sophia and Mary from Havana to La Recompensa and had visited them there. According to Mrs. Cleveland Sophia had kissed James Burroughs in front of several people. What was even worse, she had written secret letters to him and he had bragged about the letters in a tavern. What Mrs. Cleveland did not know was that Mr. Burroughs had proposed to Sophia during the voyage; she had refused him.

Mrs. Cleveland's gossip flew to Elizabeth, who wrote an angry letter to Mary. How could she have let such a thing happen? Never mind that Sophia was then twenty-five years old, she was still the sick little sister and it was Mary's duty to see that she behaved. That was Elizabeth's opinion. She also told Mary that she had checked up on James Burroughs and discovered that not only was he forty years old, he was a "brute" with an unsavory reputation.

In another letter Elizabeth told Mary that she had better get Sophia's letters back herself. She should return the gifts and letters he had sent to them with this letter: "The Miss Peabodys—thinking it important that there should remain no ground for misunderstanding . . . return to him the accompanying articles and would thank him to enclose two letters still remaining in his hands from Miss S.P. . . . the Misses P. here express their last good wishes for Mr. B's health and happiness."

Sophia did not care much about what was being said of her in Salem. She had merely kissed Burroughs on the forehead in front of other people. Wasn't that proof of her innocence? But in Cuba, where the code for proper behavior was even stricter than in New England, Mrs. Morrell was snubbing the impulsive American girl. That hurt.

The whole episode blew over gradually and had completely disappeared when Mary and Sophia sailed for home on April 29, 1835.

Sophia's headaches had not been cured in Cuba but her health had improved substantially and she fully expected the improvement to continue back in Salem. Once again she applied herself to copies of paintings which Elizabeth sold for her. Once again her desire to create her own works of art was in conflict with Elizabeth's commissions for her copies and with her own desire to be self-supporting.

"I *never* shall cease to be surprised at what I do with my pencil," she wrote to Elizabeth. "I never feel so *humble* as [when I am drawing]. . . . I do not think there is any great capacity shown in *copying*—which is all I have done yet—I have never produced anything. But I create . . . within and perhaps I shall one day shadow my images forth. . . . I shall never be happy till I *create* something."

Sophia's life was conflict ridden. She said she wanted to create but she seldom tried. No one knows how many originals she started or finished but the few that have survived do not give evidence of creative genius. Fearing to face her own limitations, she continued to copy and to dream of creating.

Her friends were assuming the accepted roles for young women of their day. Her journals are filled with reports of weddings and births. Here again was conflict for Sophia. She no doubt dreamed of a home of her own but she had been taught to fear marriage. She had been casually courted by several young men but she had only loved a doctor too many years her senior who had never proposed to her. Still she could not accept the idea of spinsterhood. Unlike her sisters she had no well-established career and had never been fully self-supporting.

Illness offered her a way to escape her conflicts. It

excused her from marriage, from earning her own way, and from trying to create. It also satisfied her mother's need for a loving child at home. So the once-spirited Sophia languished romantically in the house on Charter Street. Looking out over the adjoining graveyard, she tried to forget the here and now and focus her thoughts on the reward awaiting her in heaven.

Sophia seemed doomed to eternal childhood, always to be dependent, never to be fulfilled—like a rose blighted in the bud stage.

3

What If They Should Fall in Love?

It is difficult to imagine Elizabeth Peabody in the role of Cupid and yet it was this determined spinster who brought the slowly emerging author into the presence of the languishing invalid.

Elizabeth, who had grown ever more opinionated, more strident, and more domineering, had established herself at the very hub of Boston's intellectual and literary circles and delighted in her friendships with famous men. When her associates began to speculate about the anonymous author of "The Gentle Boy" and other stories, she resolved to discover his identity. Rumor had it that the author was named Hawthorne. Putting two and two together and coming up with five, she decided that Ebe Hathorne was just the person to have written these strange, mystic tales. The two Elizabeths had attended school together in their early childhood and Elizabeth Peabody had admired the remarkably intelligent Elizabeth Hathorne, two years her senior. Although they had probably not met since childhood, Miss Peabody must have seen the black-cloaked Miss Hathorne as she walked through the town toward the rocky coast at twilight.

So it was that Elizabeth Peabody astounded her mother and sisters by announcing that she was off to Herbert Street to lift the veil of anonymity from the literary genius hidden there. Mary was aghast. Had Miss Hathorne indicated that she wished the clouds lifted? She had not. Never mind, Elizabeth knew what was best for everyone, so she marched forth. She pounded on the door until at last Louisa appeared.

"Your sister is a genius," Miss Peabody announced without preamble.

"My brother, you mean," whispered timid Louisa.

Elizabeth was startled but not silenced. "If your brother can write like that, he has no right to be idle."

"My brother is never idle," responded the author's sister.

Elizabeth returned to Charter Street triumphant. She knew what few others knew, the identity of the author of "The Gentle Boy." She intended to share her knowledge with her friends in Salem and Boston.

A year passed. Then Elizabeth received a complimentary copy of *Twice-Told Tales* from the author. She promptly wrote her thanks. A short time later she met Louisa on the street and invited her and her sister and brother to visit the Peabody home that evening. To Elizabeth's surprise the doorbell did ring that evening and there on the doorstep stood Nathaniel Hawthorne "in all the splendor of his young beauty, and a hooded figure hanging on each arm."

All three guests were nervous and ill at ease but Elizabeth led them into the Peabody parlor and seated them around a table to examine some new, richly illustrated books that she had just received. As soon as they began to relax with the books, she excused herself and ran upstairs.

"Oh, Sophia," she exclaimed, "Mr. Hawthorne and his sisters have come, and you never saw anything so splendid—he is handsomer than Lord Byron! You must get up and dress and come down."

Sophia laughed at her sister's enthusiasm. "I think it would be rather ridiculous to get up. If he has come once, he will come again."

She was right. When the author came for a second visit, Sophia descended the stairs wearing a simple white dressing gown. Elizabeth introduced the recluse to the invalid. He was so enchanted with her smile and her low, sweet voice that he could scarcely avoid staring at her. And she? She said later that she felt such a magnetic attraction to him the first time they met that she was bewildered, almost afraid.

Even insensitive Elizabeth was aware of the current between them. *What if they should fall in love?* Impossible. Elizabeth wrote a letter to Hawthorne in which she painstakingly explained that Sophia was a hopeless invalid who could never marry.

"She is a flower to be worn in no man's Bosom," he replied.

That taken care of, Elizabeth determined to bring Hawthorne out socially. It was obvious to her that his entire family was in need of her managerial skills in helping them to emerge from their seclusion. She began by arranging for the author to be invited to an evening gathering in Salem. The hostess was Mary Foote, a longtime friend of the Peabodys and a young woman who had read the *Twice-Told Tales* with great enthusiasm. Hawthorne arrived at the Foote home and stood in the doorway, paralyzed by shyness until Elizabeth and Mary Peabody both stepped forward and took his hands and drew him into the parlor. As he began to relax, he was able to participate in the conversation. Although he spoke only short phrases, he listened so intently to what others had to say that they actually became more eloquent in his presence. The evening thus passed very pleasantly.

Somehow the Peabody sisters were able to make friends of the Hathorne sisters. The forceful Elizabeth Peabody might have intimidated the Hathornes, but after her first assault on their home to discover the author of "The Gentle Boy," she practiced restraint unusual to her. Perhaps Ebe Hathorne returned Elizabeth Peabody's admiration. If Ebe's reclusiveness was based on a sense of her own intellectual superiority, she had to be attracted to the Peabodys, who were her equals in intelligence, education—and poverty. Furthermore all three Peabody sisters were masters of the art of friendship. Unlike her older sister, Mary was a woman of quiet charm and she and Ebe seemed to have developed a special closeness. Sophia's gaiety so brightened the corners of the Herbert Street house that she was even received by Madame Hathorne. However it happened, the two sets of sisters were soon walking together, visiting in one another's homes, and exchanging notes.

Nathaniel Hawthorne too began to see a great deal of the Peabodys. Although Sophia never went out after dark because the night air was thought to be damaging to her health, Nathaniel often escorted Elizabeth and Mary to social functions in the evening. In fact he was so often in their company that some suspected he was courting Elizabeth. Elizabeth may have been among them. Certainly she was blind to the signs of a developing bond between the author and her younger sister. This was due in part to the fact that Elizabeth expected to be obeyed. She had told Hawthorne that Sophia could never marry. It would never occur to Elizabeth that he might ignore her warning. The gossip-provoking affair with Mary Silsbee and the aborted duel also took place at this time and further confused Elizabeth's vision.

When Elizabeth moved to West Newton, she received letters from both Hawthorne and Sophia. Sophia's were most revealing. She wrote that when Hawthorne came to tea on April 23, 1838, she was already in bed and too exhausted to get up and go downstairs but she opened her door and tried to hear the conversation. "Was not it a pity that I should lose such a long visit? . . . Mary said he looked very brilliant. . . . Then I must needs dream about him all night."

Three days later she had gone upstairs to lie down. She had already pulled the combs out of her hair and untied her dress. "But I had scarcely touched my cheek to the pillow when the bell rang, and I was just as sure it was Mr. Hawthorne as if I had seen him." She dressed with great haste and hurried down. She gave him a violet and he admired the mosaic she was making. "He looked very brilliant." After he was gone, she had "a delightful night" and in the morning felt "quite lark-like."

He came again the next day and again he "looked very brilliant. What a beautiful smile he has." She went on to report to Elizabeth that he prides himself on having a smile that children love. "I should think they would indeed— There is the innocence and frankness and purity of a child's soul in it. I saw him better than I had ever before."

On April 30 she reported that he had visited and "I came down to catch a glimpse of him— He has a celestial expression which I do not like to lose. It is a manifestation of the divine in human."

Between visits from Hawthorne, Sophia was kept busy trying to entertain her brother George. Wellington had died in New Orleans and George too was dying of tuberculosis of the spine. Sophia frequently went to his room to paint so that she could talk with him while she worked.

In July Hawthorne told Sophia and Mary that he was going away but he wouldn't say where. He might even change his name, he said, so that if he died no one could find his grave. He left Salem on July 23, traveled west to the Berkshires, and returned on September 24. While he was gone he kept a journal which indicated that the man who had been in deep despair just a few years earlier was now enjoying buoyant spirits. He was interested in everything: the people he met, how they lived, what they said, the little dramas of their lives, the beauties of nature. The former recluse was participating in life.

Another of Hawthorne's journals, which he kept intermittently between 1835 and 1841, was recently discovered among the papers of an old Salem family. Before his Berkshire trip he copied passages from the *Cuba Journal* into his journal. One of these is a letter from Mary to her mother describing the sleeping Sophia. After he returned from the Berkshires, he wrote about her often.

While he was gone, Sophia had read or reread his stories and made a drawing of the hero of "The Gentle Boy." She showed it to him when he returned.

"I want to know if it looks like your Ilbrahim," she said.

"He will never look otherwise to me," Hawthorne replied.

She redrew her picture for publication and Hawthorne wrote in his journal that she was so dissatisfied with the position of the boy's foot that she could not sleep "because Ilbrahim kicked her." The new edition of the story, designed for children, was a large flat book with Sophia's illustration used as a frontispiece, a dedication to Miss Sophia A. Peabody, and a long preface praising her work.

During that busy fall Sophia asked Hawthorne to sit for her and he recorded the following in his journal:

"S.A.P.—taking my likeness, I said that such changes would come over my face, that she would not know me when we met again in Heaven. 'See if I don't!' said she, smiling. There was the most peculiar and beautiful humor in the point itself, and in her manner, that can be imagined."

Later he recorded an idea for a story she had given him and then this item: " 'There is no Measure for Measure in my affections. If the Earth fails me in love, I can die and go to GOD.'—S.A.P."

Hawthorne gave Sophia a copy of his *Twice-Told Tales* which he inscribed "Miss Sophia A. Peabody, with the affectionate regards of her friend, Nath. Hawthorne. 1838." Few books have ever been so lovingly and elaborately encased as this book, which is now housed in the Berg Collection of the New York Public Library. A plain blue leather box shaped like a book has golden cupids in each corner. The top half lifts off to reveal a second blue leather book-shaped box. This box is more elaborate with an all-over floral design in gold and red and the words "All the world loves a lover." The second box is shaped on the inside to hold the simple little book and is lined with leather-framed white silk panels. Tradition has it that Hawthorne had these boxes made for Sophia to mark their betrothal. It seems more likely, however, that she in later years had them made to hold what was her most valuable possession, the copy of *Twice-Told Tales* which was his first gift to her.

◆ ◆

Sophia and Nathaniel walked together during the fall and early winter—miles and miles along the seashore and up to Gallows Hill. During one of those walks he must have declared his love. She was not a coy miss who would hang her head and blush. She obviously returned his love and no doubt told him so. But marriage was out of the question. She would not allow him to shoulder the burden of a sickly wife. True, she worked almost every day and partially supported herself with her painting, but she also depended on daily doses of morphine to relieve her pain and she spent a large part of every day in bed. He needed a healthy wife who could make a comfortable home for him; she was not fit for that. She could become fit, he said. Love was stronger than leeches or drugs and he was willing to give all the love required to cure her. While she was recuperating on his love, he would start earning money, another necessity for their marriage.

Hawthorne had been a passive Democrat for years, as were Bridge and Pierce. Through his friends he obtained a political appointment to the Boston Custom House. It was his first regular, nonliterary job. He began work on January 1, 1839, boarding ships as they came into the harbor to determine the size of the cargo and the tax to be paid.

Early in February Sophia was in Boston too. The

purpose of her visit was to check the engraving of her illustration for "The Gentle Boy." A letter written February 9 to her father is filled with news of Hawthorne, who came to see her every day.

"Before I went out in the morning Mr. Hawthorne came to see me and I had a delightful visit from him quite undisturbed. . . . After dinner . . . Mr. Hawthorne came to go with me to Mary Mosley's—but when we were on the way he said he did not want to go see anybody—and so we walked round the common and saw the sunset."

At the top of the letter she wrote a line begging her father to show it to no one, presumably her mother. Dr. Peabody seems to be more like a piece of furniture to be moved about by the Peabody women than the patriarch of his family. Nevertheless he was an affectionate father. He would rejoice to hear any news that promised a normal, happy life for his daughter.

Mrs. Peabody, on the other hand, could never welcome a romance that would loosen the mother-daughter ties essential to her happiness. However, she was so busy nursing George that she did not notice the change in Sophia, and Sophia and Dr. Peabody conspired to keep her in ignorance for as long as possible.

Hawthorne's job at the Custom House was supposed to have allowed him time to write. Write he did, but not the essays and tales his friends expected. Instead he wrote love letters to Sophia which contain some of the most beautiful passages he ever created. His first surviving letter runs to almost a thousand words. It was written on March 6 and 7, 1839, when Sophia had returned to Salem. Following are passages from it and from other letters written that spring:

". . . Do grow better and better—physically, I mean, for I protest against any spiritual improvement, until I am better able to keep pace with you—but do be strong and full of life—earthly life—and let there be a glow in your cheeks. And sleep soundly the whole night long, and get up every morning with a feeling as if you were newly created; and I pray you to lay up a stock of fresh energy every day till we meet again; so that we may walk miles and miles, without your once needing to lean upon my arm. Not but what you *shall* lean upon it, as much as you choose—indeed, whether you choose or not—but I would feel as if you did it to lighten my footsteps, not to support your own. Am I requiring you to work a miracle within yourself? Perhaps so—yet, not a greater one than I do really believe might be wrought by inward faith and outward aids. Try it, my Dove, and be as lightsome on earth as your sister doves are in the air."

". . . I invite your spirit to be with me—at any hour and as many hours as you please—but especially at the twilight hour, before I light my lamp. Are you conscious of my invitation? I bid you at that particular time, because I can see visions more vividly in the dusky glow of firelight, than either by daylight or lamplight. Come—and let me renew my spell against headache and other direful effects of the east wind. How I wish I could give you a portion of my insensibility!—And yet I should be almost afraid of some radical transformation, were I to produce a change in that respect. God made you so delicately, that it is especially unsafe to interfere with His workmanship. If my little Sophie—mine own Dove —cannot grow plump and rosy and tough and vigorous without being changed into another nature then I do think that for this short life, she had better remain just what she is. . . . I never, till now, had a friend who could give me repose;—all have disturbed me; and whether for pleasure or pain, it was still disturbance, but peace overflows from your heart into mine. . . ."

". . . my heart longed to drink your thoughts and feelings, as a parched throat for cold water. . . . I feel myself unworthy of your love. But if I am worthy of it, you will always love me; and if there be anything good and pure in me, it will be proved by my always loving you. . . ."

"*Most beloved Amelia,* I shall call you so sometimes in playfulness, and so may you; but it is not the name by which my soul recognizes you. It knows you as Sophie; but I doubt whether that is the inwardly and intensely dearest epithet either. I believe that 'Dove' is the true word after all; and it never can be used amiss, whether in sunniest gaiety or shadiest seriousness. And yet it is a sacred word, and I should not love to have anybody hear me use it, nor know that GOD has baptised you so—the baptism being for yourself and me alone. By that name, I think, I shall greet you when we meet in Heaven. Other dear ones may call you 'daughter,' 'sister,' 'Sophia,' but when, at your entrance into Heaven, or after you have been a little while there, you hear a voice say 'Dove!' then you will know that your kindred spirit has been admitted (perhaps for your sake) to the mansions of rest. That word will express his yearning for you—then to be forever satisfied; for we will melt into one another, and be close, close together then. . . ."

". . . I always feel as if your letters were too sacred to be read in the midst of people—and (you will smile) I never read them without first washing my hands! And so my poor Dove is sick, and I cannot take her to my bosom. I do really feel as if I could cure her. . . . Oh, my dearest, do let our love be powerful enough to make you well. I will have faith in its efficacy—not that it will work an immediate miracle—but it shall make you so well at heart that you cannot possibly be ill in the body. Partake of my health and strength, my beloved. Are they not your own, as well as mine? Yes—and your illness is mine as well as yours; and with all the pain it gives me, the whole world should not buy my right to share in it. . . ."

On July 17 he wrote saying he would see her on Saturday. Before that meeting they had declared their love to one another but they had spoken of marriage as something remote or impossible. At that meeting they must have decided that, come what may, they would marry. They were formally, if secretly, engaged and from that

time on Nathaniel would refer to Sophia as his "wife."
Following is an excerpt from the first letter he wrote
after his return from Salem:

"*Mine own,* I am tired this evening . . . and my head
wants its pillow—and my soul yearns for the friend
whom God has given it—whose soul He has married to
my soul. Oh, my dearest, how that thought thrills me!
We *are* married! I felt it long ago; and sometimes, when
I was seeking for some fondest word, it has been on my
lips to call you—'Wife'! . . . Often, while holding you
in my arms, I have silently given myself to you, and
received you for my portion of human love and happiness, and have prayed Him to consecrate and bless the
union. . . . My beloved, why should we be silent to one
another—why should our lips be silent—any longer on
this subject? The world might, as yet, misjudge us; and
therefore we will not speak to the world; but why
should we not commune together about all our hopes of
earthly and external as well [as] our faith in inward
and eternal union? Farewell for tonight, my dearest—
my soul's bride!"

The world to whom they feared to reveal their engagement actually consisted of only three women: Mrs.
Peabody, Madame Hathorne, and Ebe. Mrs. Peabody
was so preoccupied with George's final illness that it
was probably kind to keep the upsetting news from her.
Hawthorne had always been in awe of sharp-tongued
Ebe, who had told her brother that their mother was
too frail to withstand the shock of her only son's mar-

riage. Such was not the case: Madame Hathorne had become fond of the young woman who had brought gaiety and life into their home and would have welcomed her as a daughter-in-law, but since mother and son never discussed matters of importance, he did not know how she felt.

Sophia stated her position about the romance very clearly: "If God intends us to marry, He will let me be cured. If not, it will be a sign that it is not best." Then she went on to write letters that were just as open and passionate as his. Unfortunately only three of her letters remain as testimony of her love. Years later Hawthorne wrote in his journal that he had burned heaps of old letters and papers. "Among them were hundreds of Sophia's maiden letters—the world has no more such; and now they are all ashes. What a trustful guardian of secret matters fire is!"

Sophia kept Nathaniel's letters. Passages from three he wrote in August and September of 1839 follow:

". . . Force your way through the mists and vapors that envelope my slumbers—illumine me with a radiance that shall not vanish when I awake. I throw my heart as wide open to you as I can. Come and rest within it, Dove. . . . Dearest, I could almost think that the institution of marriage was ordained, first of all, for you and me, and for you and me alone; it seems so fresh and new— so unlike anything that the people around us enjoy or are acquainted with. Nobody ever had a wife but me—nobody a husband, save my Dove. . . ."

". . . My beloved, you make a Heaven round about you, and dwell in it continually; and as it is your Heaven, so is it mine. . . . Oh, beloved, if we had but a cottage somewhere beyond the sway of the east wind, yet within the limits of New England, where we could be always together, and have a place to *be* in—what could we desire more? . . . And you should draw, and paint, and sculpture, and make music, and poetry too, and your husband would admire and criticise; and I, being pervaded with your spirit, would write beautifully and make myself famous for your sake, because perhaps you would like to have the world acknowledge me—but if the whole world glorified me with one voice, it would be a meed of little value in comparison with my wife's smile and kiss. . . ."

". . . I have observed that butterflies . . . frequently come on board of the salt ship when I am at work. What have these bright strangers to do on Long Wharf, where there are no flowers or any green thing. . . . I cannot account for them, unless, dearest, they are the lovely fantasies of your mind, which you send thither in search of me. . . ."

Hawthorne interspersed his poetic love lines with homely—often humorous sentences about his day-to-day life. He obviously enjoyed his hard physical labor and his associations with working-class men on the docks. In April he reported that he had been engaged "all the forenoon in measuring twenty chaldrons of coal —which dull occupation was enlivened by frequent brawls and amicable discussions with a crew of funny little Frenchmen from Acadie." The following February he wrote as follows:

". . . Your husband has been measuring coal all day, aboard of a black little British schooner, in a dismal dock at the north end of the city. Most of the time, he paced the deck to keep himself warm. . . . The vessel lying deep between two wharves, there was no more delightful prospect, on the right hand and on the left, than the posts and timbers, half immersed in the water, and covered with ice, which the rising and falling of successive tides had left upon them; so that they looked like immense icicles. Across the water, however, not more than half a mile off, appeared the Bunker Hill monument; and what interested me considerably more, a church-steeple, with the dial of a clock upon it, whereby I was enabled to measure the march of the weary hours. Sometimes your husband descended into the dirty little cabin of the schooner, and warmed himself by a red-hot stove, among biscuit-barrels, pots and kettles, sea-chests, and innumerable lumber of all sorts. . . ."

He went often to visit Mary Peabody, and friends came to visit him.

". . . a little before nine o'clock John Forrester and Cousin Haley came in, both of whom I so fascinated with my delectable conversation that they did not take leave till after eleven." Still, he was not comfortable in society. He told Sophia that he had been invited to dinner to meet Margaret Fuller (a feminist writer and lecturer whose path was to cross his many times during their lives) but "Providence had given me some business to do; for which I was very thankful. When my Dove and Sophie Hawthorne can go with me, I shall not be afraid to accept invitations to meet literary lions and lionesses, because then I shall put the above-said redoubtable little personage in front of the battle. . . ."

Two weeks later he said he had been invited to go to Dr. Channings's. "What is to be done? Anything, rather than to go. I never will venture into company, unless I can put myself under the protection of Sophie Hawthorne. . . ." Earlier he had refused a ticket to a lecture by Ralph Waldo Emerson. The recluse of Herbert Street was still too introverted to enjoy crowds of people, no matter how distinguished they might be.

Back in Salem, George was growing worse and Sophia was racing the angel of death to prepare a clay model of his head. When the model was done, Sophia and her father took it to Boston where it was cast in permanent plaster. She had been well satisfied with the model but she was disappointed in the final cast. In making the cast, the clay form was broken so there was nothing to be done but to take the cast away and work on it with a knife to try to improve it.

While in Boston she also went shopping with Nathaniel. He had rented rooms in the home of his friend George Hillard and his wife. Mary had promised to help him select furniture but when she became ill, Sophia filled in for her at her school and also as an assistant shopper. Together she and Hawthorne bought a beautiful carpet with a deep garnet-colored background. "Tell Mary it cost not one cent more than the small figured ugly one at which she and Mrs. Hillard looked," Sophia wrote to George.

After her return to Salem, Sophia received a letter in which Hawthorne extolled the beauties of that carpet:

". . . what a beautiful carpet did you choose for me! I admire it so much that I can hardly bear to tread upon it. It is fit only to be knelt upon. . . . Many times today have I found myself gazing at it; and I am almost tempted to call in people from the street to help me admire it worthily. But perhaps they would not quite sympathize with my raptures. . . ."

George died in December and Hawthorne wrote hundreds of words of comfort to Sophia:

"Strive to fling your burthen upon me; for there is strength enough in me to bear it all, and love enough to make me happy in bearing it. . . . My bosom was made, among other purposes, for mine ownest wife to shed tears upon."

On the last day of December she wrote one of the three letters that has survived. It was sent to Hawthorne with some tightly rolled paper tapers she had made to be used in transferring fire from the stove to a candle. She had hurt her right hand and had written the letter with her left.

"Best Beloved,—I send you some allumettes wherewith to kindle the taper. There are very few, but my second finger could no longer perform extra duty. These will serve till the wounded one be healed, however. How beautiful is it to provide even this slightest convenience for you, dearest! I cannot tell you how much I love you, in this backhanded style. My love is not in this attitude, —it rather bends forward to meet you. . . ."

Three weeks later she sent him another gift, two original paintings she had created just for him. Hawthorne's response would have gratified any artist:

". . . Dearissima, there never was anything so lovely and precious in this world. . . . [The dove] flew straightway into my heart—and yet she remains just where you placed her. . . . Mine ownest, it is a very noble-looking cavalier with whom Sophie is standing on the bridge. Are you quite sure that her own husband is the companion of her walk? . . . we will talk about these pictures all our lives and longer; so there is no need that I should say all that I think and feel about them now; especially as I have yet only begun to understand and feel them. . . ."

◆ ◆

Few letters were written in the fall of 1840 because the lovers were living in the same city and seeing one another often. The Peabody family moved from Salem to Number 13 West Street in Boston, where they all lived and worked. Dr. Peabody had a small corner office on the street floor in which he saw his patients. Sophia had a room upstairs in which she could paint. Mary lived in the house but the room where she taught very young children was elsewhere.

The address was to become famous, however, because it was there that Elizabeth opened a bookstore and publishing business. The thinkers and doers of Boston met at Elizabeth's West Street shop to talk with one another and to examine the books and periodicals she ordered from Europe. Emerson, Thoreau, and Bronson Alcott were among those who gathered there. Margaret Fuller, staunchly feminist, also conducted her celebrated "Conversations," lectures for women, at the shop. Gatherings of intellectuals gave great satisfaction to Elizabeth as well as to her mother. From her rocking chair by the window Mrs. Peabody presided over the shop, selling books and directing customers' attention to Sophia Amelia Peabody's paintings, which hung on the walls. Also for sale were herbal medications prepared and bottled by young Nathaniel Peabody, now a pharmacist.

Elizabeth wrote articles for *The Dial*, a quarterly publication filled with essays by the eminent philosophers of the day. Miss Fuller and later Ralph Waldo Emerson edited the magazine and in 1841 Elizabeth became its publisher. She also published *Grandfather's Chair*, a history of New England through the Revolution written for children by Nathaniel Hawthorne. Elizabeth's enterprises were not destined for financial success but they helped to earn her a place in literary history.

Nathaniel was naturally a frequent visitor at 13 West Street, although even Sophia's attractions could not induce him to step inside the shop when the women assembled for one of Miss Fuller's lectures. All of the members of her family were by this time aware of Sophia's engagement. Even Mrs. Peabody seemed to accept it. She could do so because in her heart of hearts she was sure that her precious Sophia would never be strong enough to marry. In the meantime the handsome, mysterious author brightened her daughter's days. The engagement was futile but so romantic!

The lovers, however, were becoming increasingly dissatisfied with their long engagement. They wished to live together. Nathaniel had worked at the Boston Custom House for almost two years and he had saved a thousand dollars. That might have been enough to begin married life if he had been willing to commit himself to a lifetime of salaried employment. To marry Sophia was the strongest desire of his heart but there was another desire almost equal to it. He wished to write and he could see no way to combine coal, Sophia, and manuscripts. He therefore quit his job and went home to Salem to try to find the means of supporting a wife with his pen. His prospects seemed dismal.

In the bookshop on West Street he had heard many discussions of a proposed utopian commune to be called Brook Farm. Emerson, Alcott, Miss Fuller, and various other intellectuals were interested in it. Its idealistic founders expected to combine simple farm life with a chance for its members to grow intellectually. In his lonely room at the top of the house on Herbert Street Hawthorne began to think about Brook Farm. Would it be a place where he could not only write but provide for Sophia? What he did not consider was his own nature. Never has there been a less likely candidate for communal living. He had indeed mingled more with people since meeting Sophia and her family, but he was only sociable in contrast with his former hermitlike self. At last he decided to take what he must have seen as a last chance. Investing all of his savings, he joined Brook Farm in April 1841. It was still bitterly cold when he arrived, a good omen, he thought, since the Plymouth pilgrims had arrived in America in the midst of a snowstorm and they had prospered.

". . . through faith, I persist in believing that spring and summer will come in their due season," he wrote to Sophia. "But the unregenerated man shivers within me, and suggests a doubt whether I may not have wandered within the precincts of the Arctic circle, and chosen my heritage among everlasting snows. Dearest, provide thyself with a good stock of furs; and if thou canst obtain the skin of a polar bear, thou wilt find it a very suitable summer dress for this region." He went on to say that he had watched the cows being fed the night before. The commune had eight cows of its own and one belonging to Miss Margaret Fuller. She is very fractious, I believe, and apt to kick over the milk pail." He expected to milk for the first time that evening and expressed the hope that he could be assigned the kindliest cow in the herd.

He said he liked his "brethren in affliction" and had been assigned the best chamber in the house where he had hung Sophia's two paintings. He continued the letter the following day when he reported that he had not, after all, milked "because Mr. Ripley was afraid to trust [the cows] to my hands or me to their horns." Before breakfast he chopped hay for the cattle with such vehemence that he broke the machine within ten minutes. Then he brought in wood and replenished the fires. "After breakfast, Mr. Ripley put a four-pronged instrument into my hands, which he gave me to understand was called a pitch-fork; and . . . we all then commenced a gallant attack upon a heap of manure. . . . Dearest, I will never consent that thou come within half a mile of me, after such an encounter as that of this morning. Pray Heaven that [this] letter retain none of the fragrance with which the writer was embued." He concluded with another word about Miss Fuller's cow which had "made herself ruler of the herd, and behaves in a very tyrannical manner."

Three days later he told Sophia that he had milked a cow. The rest of the herd had rebelled against Miss Fuller's cow so that she needed the protection of humans. "So much did she impede thy husband's labors, by keeping close to him, that he found it necessary to give her two or three gentle pats with a shovel; but still she preferred to trust herself to my tender mercies, rather than venture among the horns of the herd. She is not an amiable cow; but she has a very intelligent face, and seems to be of a reflective cast of character."

Later in the month he went to Boston to visit Sophia

and returned to Brook Farm with a horrible cold, to be greeted by a storm. "Never didst thou hear anybody sneeze with such vehemence and frequency . . . sometimes I wanted to wrench off my head, and give it a great kick, like a foot-ball. This annoyance has made me endure the bad weather with even less than ordinary patience."

By May he was full of enthusiasm, referring to the manure as the "ore from our gold mine." Although the peas and potatoes were not yet up, "the grass blushes green on the slopes and hollows."

Sophia visited Hawthorne at Brook Farm that same month and soon after her return to Boston wrote that she could "see very plainly" that it was not the ideal place for him. He was a witness rather than a comrade of his associates. She said that everyone at Brook Farm worshiped him—as well they should—but "no one can love and reverence thee as does thy wife. In her heart centres the world's admiration, and from its depths sparkles up, beside, the starry foam of her own separate and incomparable love."

In spite of her insight that communal living was not for her lover she went on to say that the farm was very beautiful. "I do not desire to conceive of a greater felicity than living in a cottage built on one of those lovely sites, with thee. . . . Our Heaven is wherever we will make it."

"It is plain enough that for me there is no life without a response of life from thee," she wrote the next day.

"All my hope and peace and satisfaction lie in thy bosom. . . . Thou art literally my all-the-world, because where thou art not there is no world, but a vacuum. . . . Thou art a necessity of my nature as well as its crown of perfection and voluntary grace."

Twelve days later she wrote a letter in which she referred to Hawthorne as "my soul's star." These two letters and the one written with her left hand are all that escaped when her letters were burned.

Seeing the farm experience through Sophia's eyes, Nathaniel began to feel and express his doubts. "I think this present life of mine gives me an antipathy to pen and ink, even more than my Custom-House experience did. . . . It is my opinion, dearest, that a man's soul may be buried and perish under a dung-heap or in a furrow of the field, just as well as under a pile of money. . . . I yearn for thee unspeakably."

By August he was looking forward to the end of his "bondage." He wrote:

"Thou and I must form other plans for ourselves; for I can see few or no signs that Providence purposes to give us a home here. I am weary, weary, thrice weary of waiting so many ages. Yet what can be done? Whatever may be thy husband's gifts, he has not hitherto shown a single one that may avail to gather gold . . . when I look at the scanty avails of my past literary efforts, I do not feel authorized to expect much from the future. . . . Other persons have bought large estates and built splendid mansions with such little books as I mean to write; so perhaps it is not unreasonable to hope that mine may enable me to build a little cottage—or, at least, to buy or hire one. But I am becoming more and more convinced that we must not lean upon the community."

His spirits were sagging but he ended his letter on a happy note: "I doubt not that God has great good in store for us; for He would not have given us so much, unless He were preparing to give us a great deal more. I love thee! Thou lovest me! What present bliss! What sure and certain hope!"

He went home to Salem and to Boston to visit Sophia early in September. Three weeks later he was back in Brook Farm but in a new role. He was no longer a "cow-milker, potato-hoer and hay-raker," but a boarder, free to write all day long. He was free to write but he had not the "sense of perfect seclusion, which has always been essential to my power of producing anything."

Brook Farm, the dream of George Ripley, attracted many important visitors who were fascinated with the experiment and wished it well. In spite of good wishes and noble intentions, however, it was destined to be short-lived. Most of the participants, like Hawthorne, had little agricultural know-how and were more interested in brilliant conversation and in performing home-made theatricals—which Hawthorne found to be boring —than in trying to wrest a livelihood from the farm's poor soil.

Hawthorne left for good before the winter set in, having lost the money he had invested in the experiment. "I came to this place in one snowstorm, and shall probably leave it in another; so that my reminiscences of Brook Farm are like to be the coldest and dreariest imaginable."

———◆•◆———

For more than three years Sophia and Nathaniel had been struggling to demolish the barriers to their marriage. Neither had been successful. "If God intends us to marry, He will make me well," she had written, but God had not made her well. Her head still ached and her body had been further weakened by a recent long bout with flu. The money he had earned in Boston had been lost at Brook Farm so that he was as impecunious as ever.

During the three years, however, their love and their need for one another had grown so that the barriers to their marriage had diminished in importance. If Sophia could not be robust, she would ignore her illness and marry in spite of it. Poverty was more difficult for Nathaniel to ignore. Once content to live in solitude on very little, he now recognized his absolute need for her and his responsibility to support her.

He had to have been deeply discouraged when he returned to Salem from Brook Farm. Years earlier he had returned to Salem and sunk into so deep a depression that Bridge had feared he would take his own life. Since then he had become less self-indulgent and more resilient, so he sat down and wrote a letter to Sophia which was designed to cheer them both:

"*Truest Heart,* Here is thy husband in his old chamber, where he produced those stupendous works of fiction, which have since impressed the Universe with wonderment and awe! To this chamber, doubtless, in all succeeding ages, pilgrims will come to pay their tribute of reverence;—they will put off their shoes at the threshold, for fear of desecrating the tattered old carpet. 'There,' they will exclaim, 'is the very bed in which he slumbered, and where he was visited by those ethereal visions, which he afterward fixed forever in glowing words! There is the wash-stand, at which this exalted personage cleansed himself from the stains of earth. . . . There, in its mahogany frame, is the dressing-glass, which reflected that noble brow. . . . There is the pine table—there the old flag-bottomed chair—in which he sat, and at which he scribbled, during his agonies of inspiration! There is the old chest of drawers, in which he kept what shirts a poor author may be supposed to have possessed! There is the closet, in which was reposited his threadbare suit of black! There is the worn-out shoe-brush with which this polished writer polished his boots. There is—but I believe this will be pretty much all;—so here I close the catalogue.

"Most dear, I love thee beyond all limits, and write to thee because I cannot help it;—nevertheless, writing grows more and more an inadequate and unsatisfactory mode of revealing myself to thee. I no longer think of saying anything deep, because I feel that the deepest and truest must remain unsaid. . . ."

Loving one another "beyond all limits," the two found that letters had indeed become inadequate. The engagement had gone on too long. Hawthorne set out on a trip to New York City and Albany to line up publishers for the future products of his pen. He returned with nothing but hope and promises and rented an old house in Concord. Ignoring her ill health, Sophia agreed to marry him on June 20, 1842.

Hawthorne still had not told his sisters and mother of his engagement, so Sophia took matters into her own hands and wrote to his sisters. "Thy letter to my sisters was most beautiful," responded Hawthorne. "If they do not love thee, it will be because they have no hearts to love with; . . . They will love thee, all in good time, dearest; and we will be very happy."

A week or more passed and finally he spoke to his mother about Sophia. Mother and son had lived so close physically and so distant emotionally that it came as a surprise to the son to discover that his mother had long expected his announcement.

"Foolish me, to doubt that my mother's love would be wise, like all other genuine love! . . . It seems that our mother had seen how things were, a long time ago. At first, her heart was troubled, because she knew that much outward as well as inward fitness was requisite to secure thy foolish husband's peace; but, gradually and quietly, God has taught her that all is good; and so, thou dearest wife, we shall have her fullest blessing and concurrence. My sisters, too, begin to sympathise, as they ought; and all is well. God be praised! I thank Him on my knees, and pray him to make me worthy of thee, and of the happiness thou bringest me."

The obstacle was not the silent Hawthorne mother— or even the grudging Ebe—but the loquacious, loving Peabody mother who had appeared to accept the engagement. Once the house was rented and the wedding date set, Mrs. Peabody presumably launched a fierce attack that had to have shocked Sophia. She must have begun by discussing Sophia's health. She was simply too frail to withstand the rigors of marriage. It was proof of Nathaniel's insensitivity that he would even ask her to leave the comforts of her home. But all men were cruel and heartless. They expected things that Mrs. Peabody couldn't even mention to her innocent daughter. Babies were the result and Sophia could never survive childbirth. Concord was so far away that mother and daughter would never see one another. And on and on. . . .

Until at last Sophia was too sick to leave her bed. Three days before the wedding was to take place Nathaniel received a note from Sophia saying she was ill. Two days later Mary called on him to tell him that the wedding would have to be postponed. Mrs. Peabody no doubt expected the postponement to be indefinite; Mary suggested that a week might be sufficient to prepare her sister for those horrible rigors upon which Mrs. Peabody was dwelling.

Salem, Massachusetts, in the 1800's

ABOVE: Nathaniel Hawthorne's birthplace, Union Street, Salem

FACING PAGE, ABOVE: The Hawthorne house at Raymond, Maine

FACING PAGE, BELOW: The room in which Hawthorne was born.

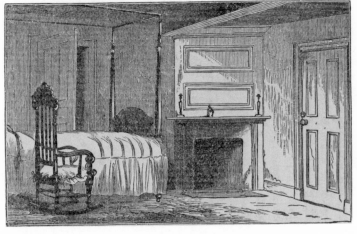

ABOVE: The "Old Manse," in Concord, Massachusetts, where
Sophia Peabody and Nathaniel Hawthorne began their
married life

FACING PAGE: Elizabeth Palmer Peabody by her
daughter, Sophia

A later Hawthorne residence in Concord, Massachusetts

4
Paradise

The first week of July 1842 was the most critical week in Sophia's life, for it was then that she was forced to choose once and for all between eternal childhood and adult responsibilities.

The pathway she had followed since girlhood was comfortable and familiar. She had enjoyed the role of the beautiful, pampered invalid and she could continue in that role. A lost love would make her even more romantic and more worthy of pity. It was a pathway that would satisfy her tender mother. At the end of the road, God the Father waited with a heavenly reward commensurate with the suffering she had known on earth.

There were no certainties along the alternate road that Nathaniel begged her to walk with him. It might descend into depths of pain or rise to heights of bliss. All she knew was that it would require stamina, for she was determined not to burden her companion but to support him, to give him peace and joy.

At last she dared to sacrifice her present quiet comfort for the adventure of traveling into the unknown with the man whom she adored.

On July 8 Hawthorne wrote to a Unitarian clergyman whom he had never met, James Freeman Clarke, and asked him to perform the marriage ceremony the next day. "Unless it should be a decidedly rainy day, a carriage will call for you at half past eleven o'clock in the forenoon."

On July 9 Sophia rose at first light and ran to the window. Although the air was filled with mist, she decided that it was not a decidedly rainy day. Her desperate mother had made her promise that she would not marry until she had been pronounced well officially, so she returned to her bed to wait for the doctor. When he at last arrived, he examined Sophia and said she was fit. His announcement must have been a severe disappointment to Mrs. Peabody. Sophia sprang from her bed and put on her wedding dress. Her friends braided her hair and adorned it with lilies.

Rain was tapping at the windowpanes as she descended the stairs and walked into the back parlor where the minister, the groom, her family, and a few close friends awaited her. But no clouds could dim her spirits as she gazed upon Nathaniel and at the moment they were pronounced man and wife, the sun broke through and flooded the small room with light.

By early afternoon the newlyweds were in the carriage on their way to Concord. Sophia described the trip to her mother in a letter that she wrote the next day. There was a shower that made the trees and shrubbery shine "like polished emerald." As for her health: "Every step the horses took, I felt better and not in the least tired. . . . My husband looked upon me as upon a mirage which could suddenly disappear. It seemed miraculous that I was so well."

The house in Concord delighted her. "Never was any fairy palace more exquisite." Neighbors had filled the rooms with welcoming flowers. She concluded by saying, "I am in tenderest keeping. Even your mother-heart would be satisfied, did it know my husband as he is." The letter is signed Sophia A. Hawthorne, perhaps the first time she had written her married name. She added a trivial postscript and signed it Sophia Amelia *Hawthorne*.

Six days later she wrote:

". . . I have continued perfectly well. . . . There was never anything so divinely quiet and lovely as the place —there never was such a charming and convenient house. . . . there never was such a husband to enrich the world since it sprang out of chaos. I feel precisely like an Eve in Paradise. We have not done much but enjoy each other. . . . We converse silently a great deal, and wonder if the earth does indeed contain such unmingled happiness and charm as we have found. . . . A limited number of hours—as I always have formerly seen him, has constrained us. It seems as if we only met to part.

But now! all our life is before us. There is no hurry— So he blooms into more consummate perfection every day —and I find that even I did not quite know him."

Sophia obviously expected her mother to share her joy, but Mrs. Peabody was more possessive than most mothers and her first letter to her married daughter was typical of those she had been writing for years. First a warning: Sophia must not love her husband exclusively but must broaden her circle of love to include others. Then a plea for sympathy:

"When any one reflects how much I have been with you for thirty years, how fully we shared each other's thoughts, how soothing in every trial was your bright smile and ready sympathy, such an one will give me credit for behaving heroically, as well as gratefully for the blessings left. My hours are fully occupied; I house-keep, paint, sew, study German, read, and give no room for useless regrets and still more useless anxieties. We are all religiously doing all we can, for ourselves and others. . . ."

Sophia realized that she would have to declare her independence from her mother, for Mrs. Peabody's sake and for her own. Her first letter after her wedding and several that followed referred to a special letter that she expected to write soon. She wrote it on August 5. "My most beloved Mother. How I wish that in a letter I could come so near you that you would not miss me at all. I wish I could be a wife and daughter at the same time so that your dear heart might not feel desolated of me." She apologized for not referring to their coming separation during her last weeks at home but she knew that such talk would have upset them both. She assured her mother of her love and wrote that she would "never cease to be grateful for the inexpressible love and devotion with which you have nursed and watched over me. Had GOD placed me with a mother one whit less tender, trustful and patient, I should not now be a living woman and the happiest wife in His universe of worlds. I owe to your sleepless care the most blissful life. . . . If my husband had not found me till I had gone to heaven, it would have been my dearest happiness to have endeavored to remunerate you by the tenderest care. . . . I bequeath my vocation now to Elizabeth and Mary. . . ."

Had her daughter stopped there in her letter, Mrs. Peabody might have been content, but Sophia did not. She went on to sing praises to her new life, away from her mother.

"There is no language to describe the fullness of my content and joy. . . . My dancing days have returned. I dance before him to the music of the musical box and of my own thoughts, and he says I deserve John the Baptist's head. You know I danced very well once. Now I can better. I have grown very 'fat and fair' and expect my face to be a full moon shortly. . . ."

The message is clear. Sophia is no longer her mother's dependent little girl but a mature woman who has at last found her identity and is standing upright beside the man she loves. Her love for her mother will always be secondary to her love for her husband.

◆•◆

The setting for their honeymoon was perfect in their eyes. Hawthorne called it the old Manse because it had previously been owned by Puritan ministers. Built in 1769 by the Reverend William Emerson, the house stands close to the historic North Bridge over the Concord River. On the morning of April 19, 1775, after Paul Revere's famous ride, British soldiers marched to Lexington and then on to Concord. There they were turned back at the North Bridge by a hastily gathered group of local farmers. Thus began the Revolutionary War. When Reverend Emerson died, another minister, Ezra Ripley, married Emerson's widow and bought the house. With the exception of the Hawthornes the occupants of the house were always to be members of the Emerson and Ripley families until 1939 when the old Manse became a historic site and was opened to the public.

A year after old Reverend Ripley died the Hawthornes rented the house furnished. They brought with them a bedroom set that Sophia had painted and decorated before her marriage, and a few other pieces. One of these was the music box that gave them such pleasure. Sophia's letters to her mother are filled with details about how they had rearranged several rooms, moving furniture from here to there.

The joy that Nathaniel and Sophia found at the old Manse is fully recorded in what must be the most per-

sonal and delightful document written in America. It is
a journal that the two of them kept together. After Nathaniel's death the aging Sophia cut out some of the
most intimate passages. Following are excerpts from
that journal interspersed with explanatory notes.

The first pages of the journal have been cut away so
that it opens with an undated entry written in Sophia's
hand sometime before August 4, 1842. After a playful
spat and a joyful reconciliation they "sat down upon the
carpet of dried pine leaves. Then I clasped him in my
arms in the lovely shade and we laid down a few moments on the bosom of dear Mother Earth. Oh how
sweet it was! . . . We walked through the field, and came
forth into an open space, whence a fair broad landscape
could be seen, our old Manse holding a respectable
place in the plain, the river opening its blue eyes here
and there and waving, mountainous ridges closing in
the horizon. . . . There seemed no movement in the
world but that of our pulses. . . . It was very lovely but
the rapture of my spirit was caused more by knowing
that my own husband was at my side than by all the
rich variety of plains, river, forest and mountain around
and at my feet."

NATHANIEL, *August 5, 1842:* "A rainy day—a rainy day
—and I do verily believe there is no sunshine in this
world except what beams from my wife's eyes. . . . Happiness has no succession of events because it is all part
of eternity; and we have been living in eternity, ever
since we came to this old Manse. . . . Externally, our
Paradise has very much that aspect of a pleasant old

domicile, on earth. The antique house (for it looks antique, though it was created by Providence expressly for
our use, and at the precise time when we wanted it)
stands behind a noble avenue of Balm of Gilead trees;
and when we chance to observe a passing traveller,
through the sunshine and the shadow of this long avenue, his figure appears too dim and remote to disturb
our sense of blissful seclusion. Few indeed, are the mortals who venture within our sacred precincts. George
Prescott . . . comes daily to bring three pints of milk,
from some ambrosial cow; . . . Mr. Emerson comes
sometimes, and has been so far favored as to be feasted . . .
on our nectar and ambrosia. Mr. Thorow* has twice
listened to the music of the spheres, which, for our private convenience, we have packed into a musical box. . . .
I must not forget to mention that the butcher comes
twice or thrice a week. . . . Would that my wife would
permit me to record the ethereal dainties that kind
Heaven provided for us. . . . Never, surely, was such
food heard of on earth—at least, not by me. . . . it is one
of the drawbacks upon our Paradise, that it contains no
water fit either to drink or to bathe in. . . . I wonder why
Providence does not cause a clear, cold fountain to
bubble up at our doorstep. . . . Only imagine Adam
trudging out of Paradise with a bucket in each hand, to
get water to drink. . . . In the way of future favors, a
kitten would be very acceptable. . . . A black dog sometimes stands at the farther extremity of the avenue, and
looks wistfully towards the house; but when I whistle to

* The Hawthornes misspelled Henry David Thoreau's name for some
time after they met him.

him, he puts his tail between his legs, and trots away. Foolish dog!—if he had more faith, he should have bones enough."

NATHANIEL, *August 6:* ". . . After breakfast, I took my fishing-rod, and went down through our orchard to the river-side. . . . This river of ours is the most sluggish stream that I ever was acquainted with. I had spent three weeks by its side, and swam across it every day, before I could determine which way its current ran; and then I was compelled to decide the question by the testimony of others. . . . it slumbers along between broad meadows, or kisses the tangled grass of mowing fields and pastures, or bathes the overhanging boughs of elder bushes, and other water-loving plants. . . . I bathe once, and often twice a day, in our river; but one dip into the salt-sea would be worth more than a whole week's soaking in such a lifeless tide. . . . I can find nothing more fit to compare it with, than one of the half torpid earthworms, which I dig up for the purpose of bait. The worm is sluggish, and so is the river—the river is muddy, and so is the worm—you hardly know whether either of them is alive or dead; but still, in the course of time, they both manage to creep away. . . ."

NATHANIEL, *August 7:* "At sunset, last evening, I ascended the hill-top opposite our house; and looking downward at the long extent of the river, it struck me that I had done it some injustice in my remarks. Perhaps, like other gentle and quiet characters, it will be better appreciated the longer I am acquainted with it. . . .

How sweet it was to draw near my own home, after having lived so long homeless in the world; for no man can know what home is, until, as he approaches it, he feels that a wife will meet him at the threshold. With thoughts like these, I descended the hill, and clambered over the stone-wall, and crossed the road, and passed up our avenue; while the quaint old house put on an aspect of welcome."

NATHANIEL, *August 8:* "I wish I could give a description of our house; for it really has a character of its own. . . . It is two stories high, with a third story of attic chambers in the gamble-roof. When I first visited the house, early in June, it looked pretty much as it did during the old clergyman's life-time, showing all the dust and disarray that might be supposed to have gathered about him, in the course of sixty years of occupancy. The rooms, I believe, had never been painted. . . . It required some energy of imagination to conceive the idea of transforming this musty edifice, where the good old minister had been writing sleepy sermons for more than half a century, into a comfortable modern residence. However, it has been successfully accomplished. The old Doctor's sleeping apartment (which was the front room on the ground floor) we have converted into a parlor; and by the aid of cheerful paint and paper, a gladsome carpet, pictures and engravings, new furniture, *bijouterie,* and a daily supply of flowers, it has become one of the prettiest and pleasantest rooms in the whole world. The shade of our departed host will never haunt it; for its aspect has been changed as completely as the scenery of a theatre. Probably the ghost gave one peep into it, uttered a groan, and vanished forever...."

Sophia, *August 10:* "Yesterday was the monthlyversary of our wedding day and quite worthy to be so for it was one of the loveliest days that ever enriched the earth. ... I am very naughty. It is inexcusable for he is the loveliest being who ever breathed life. ... This morning my darling husband brought from the river some pond lilies, pickerel weed, cardinal flowers, and one spike of arrowhead, and I put them all into the alabaster fountain."

Nathaniel, *August 10:* "The natural taste of man for the original Adam's occupation is fast developing itself in me. I find that I am a good deal interested in our garden; although, as it was planted before we came here, I do not feel the same affection for the plants as if the seed had been sown by my own hands. It is something like nursing and educating another person's children. Still, it was a very pleasant moment when I gathered the first mess of string beans. ... Almost any squash in our garden might be copied by a sculptor, and would look beautifully in marble, or in china-ware; and if I could afford it, I would have exact imitations of the real vegetable as portions of my dining-service."

Nathaniel, *August 13:* "My life, at this time is more like that of a boy, externally, than it has been since I was really a boy. ... I awake in the morning with a boyish thoughtlessness as to how the outgoings of the day are to be provided for, and its incomings rendered certain. After breakfast, I go forth into my garden, and gather whatever the bountiful Mother has made fit for our present sustenance. . . . Then I pass down through our orchard to the river-side, and ramble along its margin, in search of flowers for my wife. . . . having made up my bunch of flowers, I return with them to my wife, of whom what is loveliest among them are to me the imperfect emblems. . . . Then my dearest wife rejoices in the flowers, and hastens to give them water and arranges them so beautifully that they are glad to have been gathered from the muddy bottom of the river. . . . This important affair being disposed of, I ascend to my study, and generally read, or perchance scribble in this journal, (or, possibly, sleep!). . . . In pleasant days, the chief event of the afternoon, and the happiest one of the day, is a walk with my wife. . . . Then comes the night; and I look back upon a day spent in what the world would call idleness. . . . For a few summer-weeks, it is good to live as if this world were Heaven. And so it is, and so it shall be; although, in a little while, a flitting shadow of earthly care and toil will mingle itself with our realities."

NATHANIEL, *August 15:* "George Hillard and his wife arrived from Boston, in the dusk of Saturday evening, to spend Sunday with us. It was a pleasant sensation . . . for then I felt that I was regarded as a man with a wife and a household. . . . So my wife and I welcomed them cordially at the door, and ushered them into our parlor, and soon into the supper-room—and afterwards, in due season, to bed. Then came my dear little wife to her husband's bosom, and slept sweetly, I trust; for she is a beloved woman. . . . the night flitted over us all, and passed away, and uprose a gray and sullen morning, which would have saddened me, only that my sunny wife shone into my heart, and made it warm and bright. We had a splendid breakfast of flapjacks . . . and of whortleberries, which we gathered on a neighboring hill, and of perch, bream and pouts, which I hooked out of the river, the evening before. About nine o'clock, Hillard and I set out for a walk to Walden Pond calling by the way at Mr. Emerson's, to obtain his guidance or directions. He, from a scruple of his external conscience, detained us till after the people had got into church, and then accompanied us in his own illustrious person. . . . we proceeded through wood-paths to Walden Pond, picking blackberries of enormous size along the way. The pond itself was beautiful and refreshing to my soul. . . . After Mr. Emerson left us, Hillard and I bathed in the pond. . . . We returned home in due season for dinner, at which my wife presided with all imaginable grace and lady-likeness. . . . we sat up till after ten o'clock telling ghost-stories. . . . This morning, at seven o'clock, our friends left us. . . . we were both pleased with the visit; and so, I think, were our guests, —and pleased were we, likewise, as my dear wife is kind enough to say, to be left again to one another. . . ."

August 24: ". . . I care very little what guise the
        so complete and sufficient is my in-

ward happiness, so affective a sun of my system is my dearest lord. . . ."

SOPHIA, *August 24:* She had walked to the Alcotts with a letter for Mr. Alcott to take to Boston the next day. "I walked very diligently . . . feeling . . . strong as a little lion." After a pleasant visit Mr. Alcott's brother Junius rowed her home on the river with his nieces, Anna and Louisa. The trip "was perfectly bewitching with one great want. My noble and kingly husband should have been sitting before me with oars in hand instead of some Junius Alcott who has no place in my regard." Sophia also reported that Louisa Hathorne was visiting them.

NATHANIEL, *August 28:* ". . . In this sombre weather, when ordinary mortals almost forget that there ever was any golden sunshine, . . . my little wife seems absolutely to radiate it from her own heart and mind. The gloom cannot pervade her; she conquers it, and drives it quite out of her sphere, and creates a moral rain-bow of hope upon the blackest cloud. . . ."

NATHANIEL, *September 1:* "Mr. Thorow dined with us yesterday. He is a singular character—a young man with much of wild original nature still remaining in him. . . . He is as ugly as sin; long-nosed, queer-mouthed, and with uncouth and somewhat rustic, though courteous manners, corresponding very well with such an exterior. But his ugliness is of an honest and agreeable fashion, and becomes him much better than beauty. . . ."

for two or three years back, he has repudiated all regular modes of getting a living, and seems inclined to lead
a sort of Indian life among civilized men—an Indian
life, I mean, as respects the absence of any systematic
effort for a livelihood. He has been for sometime an
inmate of Mr. Emerson's family; and, in requital, he
labors in the garden, and performs such other offices as
may suit him. . . . Mr. Thorow is a keen and delicate
observer of nature—a genuine observer, which, I suspect, is almost as rare a character as even an original
poet; and Nature, in return for his love, seems to adopt
him as her especial child, and shows him secrets which
few others are allowed to witness. . . ."

After dinner they went down to the river and Thoreau took Hawthorne for a ride in his boat. Needing
money, he sold Hawthorne the boat "of which he is so
fit a pilot, and which he built by his own hands," for
seven dollars.

NATHANIEL, *September 2:* "Yesterday afternoon, while
my wife, and Louisa, and I were gathering the wind-
fallen apples in our orchard, Mr. Thorow arrived with
the boat. The adjacent meadow being overflowed by the
rise of the stream, he had rowed directly to the foot of
the orchard. . . . I entered the boat with him, in order to
have the benefit of a lesson in rowing and paddling. My
little wife, who was looking on, cannot feel very proud
of her husband's proficiency. . . . Mr. Thorow had assured me that it was only necessary to will the boat to
go in any particular direction, and she would immedi-

ately take that course, as if imbued with the spirit of the steersman. It may be so with him, but certainly not with me. . . . I suspect that [the boat] has not yet transferred her affections from her old master to her new one. . . . We propose to change her name from Musketaquid (the Indian name of Concord river, meaning the river of meadows) to the Pond Lily—which will be very beautiful and appropriate, as, during the summer season, she will bring home many a cargo of pond lilies. . . ."

Ellery Channing, the son of Dr. Walter Channing, called in the evening. "He is one of those queer and clever young men whom Mr. Emerson . . . is continually picking up by way of genius. There is nothing very peculiar about him—some originality and self-inspiration in his character, but none, or very little, in his intellect. Nevertheless, the lad himself seems to feel as if he were a genius; and, ridiculously enough, looks upon his own verses as too sacred to be sold for money. Prose he will sell to the highest bidder; but measured feet and jingling lines are not to be exchanged for gold—which, indeed, is not very likely to be offered for them. . . ."

Louisa's visit was a huge success; then it was Mrs. Peabody's turn to visit. That the mother was not reconciled to her daughter's health and happiness is obvious from a letter Sophia wrote just before the visit.

"My peerless mother, it sounds strangely to have you speak of being summoned to 'my sick bed'!" wrote Sophia. "I forgot that such a thing be possible. I seem to be translated out of that former Sophia Peabody's body . . . and now inhabit the fair, round, dancing, rosy, elastic form of Mistress Sophia Hawthorne. Nothing can be farther from my purpose than to be upon a sick bed."

Sophia stood firm, too, in responding to Mrs. Peabody's fears about the marriage. "You must not bring to Paradise a single anxiety—we do not entertain the Care-family at our old abbey," she wrote. "Do not fear that I shall [become] too subject to my Adam, my crown of perfection. He loves power as little [as] any mortal I ever knew. . . . His conscience is too fine and high toned to permit him to be arbitrary. His will is strong, but not to govern others. Our love is so wide and deep and equal that there could not be much difference of opinion."

Mrs. Peabody's visit was a disaster. She and Sophia did visit Emerson in his home and that gave Mrs. Peabody, a great Emerson admirer, some pleasure. Nothing else did. The weather was cold and the Manse was drafty. As might be expected, Mrs. Peabody became sick.

On September 29 Sophia was writing a letter of apology: ". . . thou dear mother, what a comfortless, sick, frozen time you had in Paradise! It is too bad. You had no delight except the witnessing of two happiest souls. Rain, wind, cough, sneezing, cold all beset you. I shall not be satisfied till you have had a good visit. . . ."

On October 9 she was still trying to explain her husband to her mother. She said that he did not like to visit. "If he had the gift of speech like some others, Mr. Emerson . . . for instance, it would be different, but he evidently was not born for mixing in general society. His vocation is to observe and not to be observed." Besides, he was hospitable and gracious to his guest and however critical Mrs. Peabody might be of him, Mr. Emerson "delights in him."

Futilely Sophia persisted in trying to convince her mother of her husband's charms and her own happiness. On November 9 she wrote, "We have the most beautiful and lovely life together. It is sweeter every day. I am perfectly well and the proud treasurer of felicity."

Pages have been removed from the old Manse journal, presumably because they referred to Mrs. Peabody's visit, and the next existing entry was made by Nathaniel.

NATHANIEL, *October 10:* "A long while, indeed, since my last date. But the weather has generally been sunny and pleasant; though often very cold; and I cannot endure to waste anything so precious as autumnal sunshine by staying in the house. . . . My chief amusement has been boating up and down the river. A week or two ago . . . I went on a pedestrian excursion with Mr. Emerson, and was gone two days and one night—it being the first and only night that I slept away from my belovedest wife. . . . After our arduous journey, we arrived safe home in the afternoon of the second day,—the first time I ever came home in my life; for I never had a home before. . . . Our apples, too, have been falling, falling, falling; and we have picked the fairest of them from the dewy grass, and put them in our store-room and elsewhere. On Thursday, John Flint began to gather those which remained on the trees; and I suppose they will amount to nearly twenty-barrels, or perhaps more. As usual, when I have anything to sell, apples are very low indeed, and will not fetch me more than a dollar a barrel. I have sold my share of the potatoe field for twenty-dollars, and ten bushels for my own use. . . ."

NATHANIEL, *November 8:* He is writing for publication and thus has little time for the journal. "During the last week, we have had three stoves put up; and henceforth, no light of a cheerful fire will gladden us at even tide. Stoves are detestable in every respect, except that they keep us perfectly comfortable."

NATHANIEL, *November 24:* "This is Thanksgiving Day —a good old festival; and my wife and I have kept it with our hearts, and besides have made good cheer upon our turkey, and pudding, and pies, and custards, although none sat at our board, but our two selves."

SOPHIA, *December 11:* "It is nearly three months since I have recorded my life and love in this journal. We have had many visitors, and have been to Boston and Salem meanwhile and various things have prevented my writing here. Last week we took our first walk together since the snow fell. . . ."

Again pages have been removed from the journal. Existing letters tell, however, of the first cloud to appear in the marriage. Sophia fell while sliding on the ice in February and subsequently had a miscarriage. It was just the disaster Mrs. Peabody had predicted and she rushed to her daughter's bedside, ready to comfort Sophia and blame Nathaniel. Sophia, however, proved to be resilient and within a few weeks wrote, "But dearest mother, does it not prove the vigorous state of my health that I have borne that extreme agony without any loss of force and rebound so instantly from it? . . . We are very happy, happier than ever."

Nathaniel's next entry in the journal demonstrates that he too was able to recover quickly from what was surely a severe disappointment to both of them.

NATHANIEL, *March 31:* ". . . One grief we have had . . . all else has been happiness. Nor did the grief penetrate to the reality of our life. We do not feel as if our promised child were taken from us forever; but only as if his coming had been delayed for a season; and that, by-and-by, we shall welcome that very same little stranger, whom we had expected to gladden our home at an earlier period. The longer we live together—the deeper we penetrate into one another and become mutually interfused—the happier we are. God will surely crown our union with children, because it fulfils the highest conditions of marriage. . . ."

NATHANIEL, *April 7:* "My belovedest wife has deserted her poor husband; she has this day gone to Boston to see her sister Mary, who is to marry Mr. Mann in two or three weeks, and then immediately to visit Europe for six months. A wagon came at about eleven o'clock to carry my Dove to the stage-house. I helped her in, and stood watching her, on the door-step, till she was out of sight. Then I betook myself to sawing and splitting wood; there being an inward inquietness, which demanded active exercise; and I sawed, I think, more briskly than ever before. . . . After my solitary dinner . . . I arose and began to record in the Journal, almost at the commencement of which I was interrupted by a visit from Mr. Thoreau, who came to return a book, and to announce his purpose of going to reside at Staten Island, as private tutor in the family of Mr. Emerson's brother. . . . On my account, I should like to have him remain here; he being one of the few persons, I think, with whom to hold intercourse is like hearing the wind among the boughs of a forest-tree; and with all this wild freedom, there is high and classic cultivation in him too. . . ."

NATHANIEL, *April 10:* ". . . What is the use of going to bed at all, in solitude? I dreamed a good deal, but to no good purpose; for all the characters and incidents have vanished. . . . Oh, these solitary meals are the dismallest part of my present experience. . . . This has been a gray day, with now and then a sprinkling of snow-flakes through the air. Surely, thou shouldst not have deserted me without manufacturing a sufficient quantity of sunshine to last till thy return! Art thou not ashamed? . . ."

NATHANIEL, *April 11:* ". . . My greatest enjoyment in bed is to extend myself cross-wise, diagonally, semi-circularly, and in all over postures that would be incompatible with a bed-fellow. I believe, too, that during my sleep, I seek thee throughout the empty vastitude of our couch. . . .

". . . [Mr. Thoreau] wanted to take a row in the boat, for the last time, perhaps, before he leaves Concord. So we emptied the water out of her, and set forth on our voyage. She leaks; but not more than she did in the autumn. . . . On our return, we boarded a large cake of ice, which was floating down the river, and were borne by it directly to our own landing-place, with the boat towing behind.

". . . To-night—to-night—yes, within an hour—this Eden, which is no Eden to a solitary Adam, will regain its Eve."

SOPHIA, *undated:* ". . . Before our marriage I knew nothing of [the body's] capacities and the truly married alone can know what a wondrous instrument it is for the purposes of the heart. . . .

". . . My heart is so full—it rises to so high a mark—it overflows so bountifully, that were there not another heart to receive my boundless love I should feel sad and aimless. . . . I feel new as the earth which is just born again. I rejoice that I am, because I am his, wholly, unreservedly his. Therefore is my life beautiful and gracious. . . ."

SOPHIA, *April 23:* ". . . Friday afternoon my dearest husband took me out in the boat. We went aground on the meadow and were nearly upset in a maelstrom beneath the red bridge. . . . My sweetest love seemed discouraged . . . while I could only laugh; for I cannot feel fear; danger I do not mind with him. . . ."

NATHANIEL, *April 26:* ". . . The lilac-shrubs, under my study-window, are almost in leaf; in two or three days more, I may put forth my hand and pluck a green bough. These lilacs appear to be very aged, and have lost the luxuriant foliage of their prime. Old age has a singular aspect in lilacs, rose-bushes and other ornamental shrubs; it seems as if such things, as they grow only for beauty, ought to flourish in immortal youth, or, at least, to die before their decrepitude. . . . Persons who can only be graceful and ornamental—who can give the world nothing but flowers—should die young, and never be seen with gray hairs and wrinkles, any more than the flower-shrubs with mossy bark and scanty foliage, like the lilacs under my window. . . . Apple-trees, on the other hand, grow old without reproach; let them live as long as they may, and contort themselves in whatever fashion they please, they are still respectable, even if they afford us only an apple or two in a season, or none at all. Human flower-shrubs, if they will grow old on earth, should, beside their lovely blossoms, bear some kind of fruit that will satisfy earthly appetites; else men will not be satisfied that the moss should gather on them.

". . . Methinks my little wife is twin-sister of the Spring; so they should greet one another tenderly; for they both are fresh and dewy, both full of hope and cheerfulness, both have bird-voices always singing out of their hearts, both are sometimes overcast with flitting mists, which only make the flowers bloom brighter. . . . I have married the Spring!—I am husband to the month of May!"

SOPHIA, *May 9:* ". . . I wish I could be Midas long enough to turn into sufficient gold for thy life's sustenance and embellishment, whatever I touch. But woe is me! I do nothing but love thee. This thou couldst not do without, but I wish more could be added. . . ."

SOPHIA, *May 19:* ". . . Father arrived, his first visit to us since our marriage. He stayed till Saturday morning 13th. . . . This week I have planted my flower garden. It is the first time I ever put any seeds into the earth. . . . It has been an inexpressible happiness to watch the coming of summer and spring step by step with such a synonym and harmonic of Nature as my husband."

SOPHIA, *May 23:* "My sister Mary was married [on May 1 to Horace Mann]. . . . I never could be reconciled to her hard labor for others and her sad countenance. Now she is entirely content. . . . Monday morning I began the bust of the noblest head in Christendom or Heatheness, [sic] that of my own dear Lord."

SOPHIA, *June 5:* ". . . We have heard from Mary Mann just a month from her departure. She says she feels 'perfect satisfaction.' This is to hear rich music. . . . She and I can now nod our heads grandly at each other in saucy

defiance and say I am as happy as you! (secretly believing *happier than*) I wish Elizabeth could take up the
wondrous tale and echo 'and I as you!' "

SOPHIA, *undated:* ". . . GOD gives us all that is of eternal worth—consummate love—perfect health—even a
lovely home—and in still addition—the power to receive friends and make them happy. Sweetest husband
—has He put a very heavy yoke on us?"

All during the spring and early summer of 1843 Nathaniel wrote at length and in depth about his vegetable
garden:

April 27: ". . . I bought a load of manure, yesterday for
six dollars. . . ."

June 2: "Last night, there came a frost, which has done
great damage to my garden. . . . It is sad that Nature
will play such tricks with us poor mortals, inviting us
with sunny smiles to confide in her, and then, when we
are entirely within her power, striking us to the heart. . . ."

June 23: ". . . The garden looks well now. . . . I am
forced, however, to carry on a continual warfare with
the squash-bugs, who, were I to let them alone for a
whole day together, would perhaps quite destroy the
prospects of the whole summer. . . . My little wife
should take shame to herself for not keeping a record of
her flower-garden. . . . I wonder, too, that she has neglected to mention the birth into this wicked world of a

little white dove—perhaps the harbinger of another birth, which, at some inscrutable period, may gladden our old abbey. . . ."

July 1: "We had our first mess of green peas (a very small one) yesterday. Every day for the last week has been tremendously hot; and our garden flourishes like Eden itself—only Adam could hardly have been doomed to contend with such a tremendous banditti of weeds."

SOPHIA, *July 9:* "This is the anniversary of our wedding day, my dearest love. . . . Our state now is one of far deeper felicity than last 9th of July. Then we had visions and dreams of Paradise. Now Paradise is here and our fairest visions stand realized before us. . . . I have not felt very well for two weeks but it is the very poetry of discomfort for I rejoice at every smallest proof that I am as ladies wish to be who love their lords—and thou art so tender and indulgent to all my whims and moans and thou dost look so radiant with satisfaction and content, that I feel as if I could bear joyfully any amount of pain or unease for thy sake. Thou never wast so sweet and lovely as now. . . . Now as thou sittest before me I think thou art of priceless beauty—ah may our little dovelet look like thee!"

NATHANIEL, *July 9:* "Dearest love, I know not what to say, and yet cannot be satisfied without marking with a word or two this holiest anniversary of our life. But life now heaves and swells beneath me like a brim-full ocean; and the endeavor to comprise any portion of it in words, is like trying to dip up the ocean in a goblet. We never were so happy as now . . . God bless us and keep us. . . ."

Ever After

The first blissful year was merely a taste of the joy they were to share during the next twenty years.

The hoped-for "dovelet," a baby girl named Una, was born on March 3, 1844. Again Mrs. Peabody's predictions proved faulty: Sophia survived pregnancy and childbirth and was soon writing to exclaim over the beauty of her daughter's eyelashes and smiles and fingers. "Every morning when I wake and find the darling lying there, or hear the sound of her soft breathing, I am filled with joy and wonder and awe."

"I am at last the regular head of a family, while you are blown about the world by every wind," Nathaniel wrote to Bridge. "I commiserate you most heartily. If you want a new feeling in this weary life, get married. It renews the world from the surface to the centre.

"I am happy to tell you that our little girl is remarkably healthy and vigorous, and promises, in the opinion of those better experienced in babies than myself, to be very pretty. For my own part, I perceive her beauty at present rather through the medium of faith than with my actual eyesight. However, she is gradually getting into shape and comeliness, and by the time when you shall have an opportunity to see her, I flatter myself she will be the prettiest young lady in the world. . . ."

———◆•◆———

During the first three years of his marriage Hawthorne wrote tales and allegories. Many of these appeared in a new collection, *Mosses from an Old Manse*. An enlarged edition of *Twice-Told Tales* was also published. Bridge sailed along the coast of Africa and came home with a journal which his friend edited and rewrote for a book, *Journal of an African Cruiser*. All of these projects made money, but not enough, and several of his publishers were slow in making their payments to the author.

It was becoming increasingly difficult to pay the modest rent on the old Manse. Furthermore members of the Ripley family wanted it for their own use. In the fall of 1845 the Hawthornes left the home where they had been so happy. The house would ever after retain the name with which Nathaniel had endowed it and several of the windows would continue to bear testimony to the joy of the lovers, for they had etched their names in the glass with the diamond in Sophia's ring.

Hawthorne needed salaried employment to provide for his family. His college friends Pierce and Bridge, and O'Sullivan, with whom he had come so close to dueling, were all active Democrats. They set out to obtain a political appointment for the author. Since Hawthorne had never been a political person—it was rumored that he did not even vote—the task was not easy. Nevertheless Hawthorne moved his family into his mother's dismal home in Salem and his faith in his friends was at last rewarded with an appointment. He was named surveyor for the Port of Salem. The job was not demanding and the pay was adequate to their needs.

The next three years were marked by several moves and by the birth of a son, Julian, in June 1846. On the few occasions when Sophia visited her parents in Boston, Nathaniel wrote letters that demonstrated that his passion for her increased as the years passed:

". . . Now I have nothing to tell thee, belovedest wife, but write thee just a word, because I must. Thou growest more and more absolutely essential to me, every day we live. I never knew how thou art intertwined with my being, till this absence. . . ."

In 1849 Sophia rose to heights of heroism that could not have been dreamed of by those who had only known her in her romantic invalid days. All of the Hawthornes—including Nathaniel's mother and sister— were living in a large house on Mall Street in Salem. At the very top of the house was a secluded room for Nathaniel. He should have been able to write, away from the distractions of his family, but he could not. He was so discouraged by his inability to produce anything of literary quality that Sophia warned Elizabeth and Mrs. Peabody not to even mention his work in their letters.

Then one day in June he came home from the docks

early. He had lost his job; Whigs had won a recent election from the Democrats and had named one of their supporters to his office. His gloom can only be imagined—to lose his regular paycheck at a time when he was making nothing with his pen.

"Then you can write your book," Sophia exclaimed happily when she heard his news.

He must have thought her demented as he carefully explained all of their needs for money. She listened and then led him to her desk, threw open a drawer, and displayed a collection of gold pieces. Some of these she had saved from the sum he gave her for household expenses. The rest she had earned painting parchment lampshades and fire screens which Elizabeth had sold for her for five and ten dollars each. They would live off this money, which she had been hoarding for just such an emergency, while he wrote. That very afternoon he started work on what was originally intended as a short story but which grew to be his most famous novel, *The Scarlet Letter*.

His work was interrupted the next month when Madame Hathorne became seriously ill. In other households the man of the family would continue to work while the women cared for the sick; the Hawthornes had always been different. Sophia nursed the old lady while Nathaniel assisted the servant in caring for the children. What Ebe and Louisa did, if anything, is not clear. Ebe had become ever more reclusive—during the months they had all lived together in the house on Herbert Street, Sophia said that she had only seen Ebe once —so she probably stayed in her room. Louisa was known to be devoted to the children and perhaps she helped to care for them while Sophia was busy upstairs.

For some time Nathaniel had been writing a journal about the children's day-to-day lives. He was amazingly detached for so doting a father and reported their naughtiness as well as their sweetness. He had to have been shocked at their innocent brutality as they played dying-grandmother-and-doctor, but he recorded their words and actions faithfully:

". . . Una is transformed into grandmamma. . . . She groans, and speaks with difficulty, and moves herself feebly and wearisomely—then lies perfectly still, as if in an insensible state. Then rouses herself, and calls for wine. Then lies down on her back, with clasped hands —then puts them to her head . . . out of the midst of it, little Una looks at me with a smile of glee. . . ."

Just before his mother's death on July 31 Hawthorne wrote about one of his last visits to her bedside.

"I love my mother; but there has been, ever since boyhood, a sort of coldness of intercourse between us, such as is apt to come between persons of strong feelings if they are not managed rightly. . . . I found the tears slowly gathering in my eyes. I tried to keep them down, but it would not be; I kept filling up, till, for a few moments, I shook with sobs. For a long time I knelt there, holding her hand; and surely it is the darkest hour I ever lived."

· · ·

Three years after her mother's death Louisa died when a Hudson River steamboat on which she was traveling caught fire and exploded. Ebe lived as a paying guest with a farmer's family on the coast of Massachusetts for thirty years until her death, a recluse to the end.

By September the author was back at his desk writing all day, every day. He finished the tale in February and told Bridge that when he read the ending to Sophia, it broke her heart and sent her to bed with a headache, "which I look upon as a triumphant success."

Set in the early days of the Boston colony and peopled with punishing Puritans, *The Scarlet Letter* is a somber tale of four characters caught in a tide of sin, guilt, and revenge.

When Hester Prynne is tried for adultery and refuses to name her partner in guilt, the Puritan magistrates sentence her to a term in prison, where her baby is born. They also demand that she wear a red letter *A* on her bosom for the rest of her life. She faces her punishment with dignity and in time earns the respect of her neighbors.

Arthur Dimmesdale, the young clergyman who fathered Hester's child, appears to his congregation as a saint, zealous in the pursuit of "God's glory and man's welfare." The secret sin festering in his soul torments his spirit and weakens his body.

The old man whom Hester had married without love arrives in Boston to find his wife disgraced. He ignores her and introduces himself to the colonists as Roger Chillingworth. Although he feels that the scarlet letter is sufficient punishment for his wife, this once quiet, scholarly man becomes obsessed with his desire to discover and punish her lover.

As the novel moves toward an inevitable conclusion, the baby Pearl grows into a strange, elfin child whom her mother fears may be possessed of the devil.

James T. Fields, a partner in the publishing house of Ticknor, Reed and Fields, visited the Hawthornes in December 1849 and was shown a portion of the manuscript. Early in 1850 he received the completed manuscript which was published along with an essay entitled "The Custom House" on March 16.

Hawthorne feared that the public would be repelled by a novel that had not one glimmer of humor, but the first edition of two thousand copies was sold out in ten days. A few critics complained about the book's unrelieved gloom and others about the corrupting influence of a book about adultery, but most critics were lavish in their praise. *The Scarlet Letter* was recognized immediately as a work of genius. Today it is considered to be the first great American novel and one of the greatest novels written in the English language.

As for the accompanying essay it was considered praiseworthy and amusing by all except Salemites, who were enraged by it. Partly as a result of Salem's anger the Hawthornes moved to Lenox in western Massachusetts.

There Hawthorne wrote his second great novel, *The House of the Seven Gables*. This story of a family curse begins in the early days of Salem, where a simple man named Matthew Maule built a humble cottage on land made especially desirable because it was the site of a pure and abundant spring. Another, much wealthier man named Colonel Pyncheon believed that he had a legitimate right to the land. Old Maule, however, refused to acknowledge the colonel's claim. When Maule was eventually hanged for witchcraft, he stood on the scaffold, pointed to the colonel, and said, "God will give him blood to drink."

Undaunted, the colonel took over Maule's land and began to build a fine seven-gabled mansion on it. When the cellar was dug and the foundations laid, the sweet spring turned brackish. On the day that the house was to be consecrated, the colonel was found dead in his new study. Thus began the history of the house of seven gables and the cursed Pyncheon family. The main part of the story takes place almost two hundred years later and concerns four members of the Pyncheon family still living under the curse of old Maule.

The idea of a witch cursing an enemy and his family obviously originated with Hawthorne's own family. The house of seven gables was probably a composite of several similar houses in Salem. The story itself is the product of Hawthorne's imagination. He himself thought this a better novel than *The Scarlet Letter*. It is certainly better balanced. Although the plot is essentially grim, the book contains humor and ends happily. When it was published by Fields in April 1851, *The House of Seven Gables* was praised more lavishly than *The Scarlet Letter* and sold more quickly. Modern critics, however, generally rate the first novel above the second.

During 1851 Hawthorne also wrote *A Wonder-Book for Boys and Girls, The Snow Image and Other Twice-Told Tales*, and began a third novel. Sophia was also productive. "Mrs. Hawthorne published a little work two months ago, which still lies in sheets, but I assure you it makes some noise in the world," Hawthorne wrote to his friend Bridge to announce the birth of their third and final child, Rose.

Late in the year they returned to eastern Massachusetts where they occupied the Manns' home in West Newton. Horace Mann was serving in Congress and had moved Mary and their three young sons to Washington temporarily. Hawthorne finished *The Blithedale Romance* in West Newton. This novel, based on his experiences at Brook Farm, is interesting mainly for what he had to say about one communal living group in particular and about reformers in general. Few critics then or now have been enthusiastic about *The Blithedale Romance* but Hawthorne is to be credited with boldness. Having achieved success with his first two novels, which have almost nothing in common with one another, he might have returned to the time, place, or theme of either one of them for his third novel. Instead he tried something new.

While living in the Mann house, the Hawthornes were looking for a house to buy. At last they found it in Concord, the town where they had begun their life together. It was an old farmhouse, previously occupied by the Alcott family. Hawthorne named it The Wayside. It was the only home they were ever to own. There Nathaniel wrote *Tanglewood Tales* and a campaign biography of his old college friend Franklin Pierce, the Democratic candidate for the presidency. Thus ended the four most productive years of Hawthorne's life, during which he wrote three novels and four other books.

———◆•◆———

Even though Hawthorne was now a brilliant and famous author both at home and abroad, he was not financially secure. He never received great sums for any of his books. As he neared fifty and looked at his three young children, for whom he wished to provide a secure future, he felt the need for more money than he could earn with his pen. Once again he sought salaried employment. When Pierce was elected, he rewarded his friend and biographer with the consulship of Liverpool.

The Hawthornes sailed for England on July 6, 1853. They lived in England during Pierce's single term as president. For what seems to be the first time in her married life, Sophia was seriously ill and it was thought best that she and the girls should spend the winter of 1856 in sunny Portugal where O'Sullivan was United States minister to the Court of Lisbon. During this long separation Nathaniel wrote to her of his still ardent love:

"Thy letter, my own most beloved, . . . arrived yesterday, and revived me at once out of a state of half-torpor, half misery—just as much of each as could co-exist with the other. Do not think that I am always in that state;

but one thing, dearest, I have been most thoroughly taught by this separation—that is, the absolute necessity of expression. I must tell thee I love thee. I must be told that thou lovest me. It must be said in words and symbolized with caresses; or else, at last, imprisoned Love will go frantic, and tear all to pieces the heart that holds it. . . ."

When his term in Liverpool ended, Hawthorne took his family through France to Italy, where they lived for about a year and a half. There he wrote the first drafts of his fourth novel, *The Marble Faun*. It was completed in England, to which the family returned for a number of months in 1859.

Hawthorne was fascinated by, if not completely enamored with, the city of Rome. His puritan soul was outraged by nude statues and by the noise and filth of the city. At the same time he was impressed with the majesty of the art and intrigued by some aspects of Catholicism. *The Marble Faun*, completely different from his other three novels, is a complex tale about the loss of innocence. It contains supernatural elements, descriptions of actual artworks, and a large cast of characters including several American artists living in Rome. The book was published simultaneously in England and America and was well received in both countries.

Finally in the summer of 1860, after an absence of seven years, the Hawthornes returned to Concord. During their absence The Wayside had been occupied for a time by Sophia's brother Nathaniel and his family and then by her sister Mary Mann and her three sons.

Horace Mann had given up his law practice to become the first secretary of education for the state of Massachusetts. Influenced in part by the enthusiasm of Elizabeth and Mary Peabody, he had become an evangelist for the cause of public school education and had traveled throughout Massachusetts inspiring local communities to build and equip schools and to improve the quality of education for all children. He is credited with the establishment of the first teacher-training programs. When at last he and Mary had married in 1843, their honeymoon in Europe had been spent observing schools. After serving in Congress, he received his party's nomination for governor of Massachusetts in 1852. At the same time, he was asked to serve as the first president of a new college to open in the wilderness of Ohio. First and foremost an educator, Mann chose to become the founding president of Antioch, one of the first nonsectarian coeducational colleges in the United States. He died at Antioch in 1859 and Mary and her sons returned to the East. Mary spent the rest of her life spreading her husband's ideas about education. At the age of eighty she wrote her first novel, a romance based on her experiences in Cuba. When the book was finished, she died.

Elizabeth Peabody lived to be ninety, an activist to the end. During her lifetime she fought for kindergartens, public schools, the abolition of slavery, and women's rights. Mary Mann shared many of her elder sister's enthusiasms and the two grew closer as they grew older. Sophia, on the other hand, grew away from them. Elizabeth and Mary were fiercely opposed to slavery while Sophia was loyal to her husband who was in turn loyal to his friend Pierce. Many abolitionists considered Pierce a traitor because as president he had tried to placate southern slave owners. This political and social rift in no way diminished the love the sisters felt for one another, but it strained their ordinary relationships.

When the Hawthornes returned to Concord, they added an absurd Italian-style tower to their plain old American-style farmhouse and settled down. Hawthorne wrote ten sketches of life in England which were published in *The Atlantic* and then in a book entitled *Our Old Home*. He also wrote magazine pieces about the Civil War and started—but did not finish—several novels.

Nathaniel was seriously ill in 1863 and by the spring of 1864 he was so wasted and drawn that the only hope of relief was thought to be a trip. Travel had always refreshed him in the past. Franklin Pierce, a drab and unpopular president, was ever a loyal friend. He came to take Nathaniel on what was to be his last trip. They traveled for several days to Plymouth, New Hampshire, where Hawthorne died peacefully in a hotel on May 19, 1864.

Pierce brought the body home to Concord to be buried in Sleepy Hollow Cemetery and accompanied Sophia and the children to the funeral and the burial. Pallbearers included some of the most distinguished men of American letters: Henry Wadsworth Longfellow, James Russell Lowell, Ralph Waldo Emerson, Oliver Wendell Holmes, and Bronson Alcott.

———◆◆———

Sophia and the children continued to live at The Wayside for four years. Hawthorne had made a valiant effort to provide for his family but he had been unsuccessful. Pierce contributed to Julian's expenses at Harvard. Finally, hoping to live more cheaply in Europe than they could live at The Wayside, they moved to Dresden, Germany, in 1868 and then to London in 1870.

Sophia was comforted in her widowhood by her children and by the task she set for herself. She edited Hawthorne's journals for publication. She has been frequently criticized for deleting, rearranging, and rewriting his words but she was motivated by an obvious desire to present her husband to the world in the most favorable light. The work gave her great joy. Her hours "sang," she wrote to Fields, as she relived the early days of their marriage.

Years earlier he had written about their meeting someday in heaven, when he would call to his Dove and they would "melt into one another and be close." Soon after his death she wrote, "I have an eternity, thank God, in which to know him more and more, or I should die in despair."

When death called her in 1871 at the age of sixty-one, she went happily, sure that she would spend eternity with her "soul's star." She was buried in London under a white marble headstone which said simply, "Sophia, wife of Nathaniel Hawthorne."

———— ◆•◆ ————

Although Nathaniel Hawthorne was buried in Concord and Sophia across the ocean in London, it is to Salem that pilgrims travel to pay homage to America's great novelist. There lies the grave of the cursed Judge Hathorne next to the plain white house on Charter Street where Sophia first saw the man through whom she would find health and fulfillment. Families still live in the house on Herbert Street where he spent his years of seclusion and in the house on Mall Street where he wrote *The Scarlet Letter*. Tourists walk through the house where he was born, the house said to be the original house of the seven gables and the Custom House where he worked.

As for the witches it is hoped that they have found peace as thousands of tourists come each year to the Salem Witch Museum to hear their story.

Author's Note

Since they could only communicate face to face or through letters, it is not remarkable that Sophia and Nathaniel Hawthorne, members of their families, and their friends wrote thousands of letters to one another. What is remarkable is that so many of their letters—as well as their personal journals—have survived the passage of time. Several scholars have set out to collect transcriptions of all of Hawthorne's letters, only to be defeated by the enormity of the task. Nevertheless the yellow and fading letters are available in libraries and collections.

Hundreds of Sophia's letters, her journals, and a few of her drawings are now housed together in the Henry W. and Albert A. Berg Collection of the New York Public Library—Astor, Lenox, and Tilden foundations. There too are letters by and to other members of the Peabody family and some of the letters written by Nathaniel and his family. All of the quotations in Chapter II of this book and many of those attributed to Sophia in Chapters III and IV are from documents in the Berg Collection. Many have never before been printed. My special thanks go to the staff of the Berg Collection for making these papers available to me and for permission to quote from them.

Nathaniel Hawthorne's love letters to Sophia are now the property of the Huntington Library in San Marino, California. Sophia herself edited these letters, often cutting away and deleting portions she considered to be too intimate for the eyes of strangers. *Love Letters of Nathaniel Hawthorne* was first printed privately in 1907 for members of the Society of the Dofobs (Damned Old Fools Over Books) in an edition of only sixty-two copies. The Dofobs edition was reprinted in 1972 by NCR/ Microcard Editions, which also contains an introduction by C. E. Frazer Clark, Jr., and some of the passages from the original letters which Sophia inked out but which modern scholars have been able to restore. I used the NCR Edition in preparing this book.

All of Hawthorne's known notebooks are the property of the Pierpont Morgan Library in New York City. Soon after her husband's death, Sophia prepared portions of these notebooks for publication in *The Atlantic Monthly* and in book form. Ohio State University Press in 1972 published *The American Notebooks*, edited by Claude M. Simpson, with complete transcriptions of the existing Hawthorne notebooks and Sophia's representation of the notebooks thought to be lost. One of the

"lost" notebooks was later discovered by Mrs. Barbara
S. Mouffe, and the Pennsylvania State University Press
in 1978 published it in a facsimile edition with a
transcription by Mrs. Mouffe in *Hawthorne's Lost Note-
book, 1835–1841*. I have quoted from both of these
printed works. Sophia's entries in the old Manse note-
book have not previously appeared in print, and I am
grateful to the Morgan Library for permission to include extracts from them.

The Essex Institute in Salem is yet another storehouse
of Hawthorne and Peabody material. Most of the boyhood letters from which I have quoted are in the Essex
Institute. I am grateful to that institution for permission
to quote, for information about early Salem, and for
showing me two of Sophia's oil paintings.

A New England Love Story is illustrated with repro-
ductions of old drawings and etchings. The pictures of
Sophia and Nathaniel are from etchings by S. A. Schoff
that appeared in *Nathaniel Hawthorne and His Wife* by
Julian Hawthorne, published in 1884. All of the other
illustrations are from the New York Public Library—
Astor, Lenox, and Tilden foundations. Sophia's drawing
of her mother is from a sketch book in the Henry W.
and Albert A. Berg Collection. The view of Salem is
from the Stokes Collection. The other illustrations are
from the Picture Collection.

In addition to the volumes already mentioned I have
found the following books to have been particularly
helpful:

HORATIO BRIDGE, *Personal Recollections of Nathaniel Hawthorne*, 1893

ESSEX INSTITUTE HISTORICAL COLLECTIONS, *Special Hawthorne Issues*, July 1958 and October 1964

JULIAN HAWTHORNE, *Nathaniel Hawthorne and His Wife*, originally published 1884; reprinted by Archon Books, 1969

GEORGE P. LATHROP, *A Study of Hawthorne*, 1876

ROSE HAWTHORNE LATHROP, *Memories of Hawthorne*, 1897

VERNON LOGGINS, *The Hawthornes*, Columbia University Press, 1951

RANDALL STEWART, *Nathaniel Hawthorne: A Biography*, originally published by Yale University Press, 1948, reprinted by Archon Books, 1971

LOUISE HALL THARP, *The Peabody Sisters of Salem*, Little, Brown and Co., 1950

Finally I wish to thank my neighbor, Francis Nielsen, for sharing with me his insights about Hawthorne and his appreciative understanding of Hawthorne's work.

LouAnn Gaeddert, 1980

ABOUT THE AUTHOR

LouAnn Gaeddert says she thoroughly enjoyed the process of gathering information for *A New England Love Story*—going through faded letters and journals; visiting Salem, Concord, and Boston; researching nineteenth-century New England history and literature.

Ms. Gaeddert is the author of a number of books for young people, including *Gustav the Gourmet Giant* (Dial). She was born in the Midwest and educated in California and Seattle. She and her husband live in New York. They have two children, who are both now in college.